# BECOMING A CONSCIOUS BUSINESS

Expand Your Life & Work Through
the Science of Energy Flow

**SAMUEL P. CHIN**

**To Emma Watson,**
*who I hope leaves this book
in the subway someday*

# DOWNLOAD THE AUDIOBOOK FREE!

Just to say thanks for purchasing my book, I would like to give you the Audiobook version **100% FREE!**

**CAVICONSULTING.COM/FREE-AUDIOBOOK**

Copyright © 2018 by Samuel P. Chin
All rights reserved. This book or any portion thereof
may not be reproduced or used in any manner whatsoever
without the express written permission of the publisher
except for the use of brief quotations in a book review.

Printed in the United States of America

First Printing, 2018

eBook ISBN 978-1-7323956-0-2
Audio Book ISBN 978-1-7323956-2-6
Paperback ISBN 978-1-7323956-1-9

LCCN 2018906749

http://caviconsulting.com

Edited by Bridget Randolph, Christina Chin, and Judi Blaze.

The advice and strategies found within this book may not be suitable
for every situation. This work is sold with the understanding that
neither the author nor the publisher are held responsible for the results
accrued from the advice in this book.

15 **Introduction**

21 **Nature's Flow**
22 **VIDEO GAMES**
26 **SCIENCE**
33 **WATER**
36 **ONENESS**

49 **Human Flow**
50 **THINKING**
58 **KNOWING**
65 **DIVORCE**
84 **PURPOSE**

91 **Business Flow**
92 **EVOLUTION**
101 **OPERATIONS**
107 **PROJECTS**
114 **IMPROVEMENT**
130 **BABIES**

137 **Conclusion**

## FOREWORD

When people ask me "So, how do you know Sam?", I'm never sure what to say. Technically I know Sam because we're family – our mothers are sisters, and we used to play together as children. But by the time I moved to New York City in 2016, we hadn't spoken in over a decade.

On the basis of our – at this point – tenuous family connection, Sam invited me to crash with him for a week or two while I was getting settled and finding a place to live; and to the surprise of both of us, I basically never left.

It was in that apartment that the seeds for this book (and the business which inspired it) were planted; although on that first night, when I arrived jetlagged at my cousin's place ready to crash after a long flight from London, I had no idea that this was where we'd end up less than two years later. This reflects the sort of serendipity and expansion which happens naturally as one becomes more aware of the energetic patterns of the universe, patterns which Sam explains so eloquently in this book.

I remember when Sam first completed the outline of the book draft. The first thing he said to me was, "I've figured out the meaning of life!". Of course I teased him at the time for his exuberance, but when I finally read the manuscript, I began to understand what he had meant.

This is a book about business, yes. But it also is about nature, creation, evolution, the flow of energy, finding love and joy, overcoming fear and ultimately, understanding the purpose and behavior of all living things within the greater patterns of the universe. (No big deal!) It is a personal story ... and also the story of everything.

This book is a scientific text told through the lens of individual experience. If you are looking for a business tactics guidebook or self improvement advice, you might do better to pick up the latest work by Seth Godin or Simon Sinek. And if you are looking for a book on spirituality, I'm sure that Sam himself would be the first to direct you to the work of Eckhart Tolle (and others like him).

What you will learn from this book, however, is a new way of viewing the world and building a business through tapping into the energetic flow of the universe – unlocking your own process vision, as Sam calls it. When we start to look at life from the perspective of that energy flow, everything becomes simple. And, in the process, we learn more about what it means to be part of nature, what it means to be human, and how businesses are the next stage of the universe's evolution towards ever-more complex form.

Sam's academic background as a biologist has informed his work as a process scientist and a student of human nature. The first part of this book is all about nature and the evolution of living forms, from the Big Bang right up to humanity and a higher form of consciousness. In this section, Sam describes how nature is designed to always optimize its own processes for creating the most value possible, and how this natural (organic) optimization eventually developed into human form, bringing in a new era of life on this planet.

In the second section, Sam focuses on the human experience and our own personal growth. Applying these evolutionary principles of value optimization to our personal lives, we begin to see how the same universal energy that flows through nature can inspire our growth as individuals (overcoming our innate fear of the unknown to embrace transparency, presence and love). But it doesn't stop there.

As humans, when we begin to bond with one another and come together in creating social structures and other organizations, we set the stage for the next phase of the evolutionary process – the rise of the business as a living organism with a will and consciousness of its own. This leads us into the third, and final, section of the book: an understanding of business as a living entity. This understanding is what enables us to most effectively remove the obstacles that prevent energy from flowing through and expanding the business organism to its full potential. This is how we "raise" our baby businesses to full maturity, finding a sense of personal fulfillment in the process.

You might be thinking, this all sounds well and good, but does it work?

The scientific method outlined in this book is not just theory. The principles and frameworks that Sam describes are the result of years of experimentation and real world application in a variety of industries and organizations, culminating in the creation of our own business: Cavi Consulting.

Cavi Consulting, which grew out of a collaboration between Sam, myself, and our friend and co-founder Hassan Khan, is a model for this new way of approaching entrepreneurship and business growth. Through the experience of becoming a business ourselves, as well as in our work with clients, we have seen firsthand the many ways in which a business can start to become its fullest self by rebalancing and removing obstacles to its natural energy flow.

It is our hope that with this book, even more businesses — and the people who comprise (and love) them — will be better able to thrive and achieve their highest potential.

**Bridget Randolph**
Manhattan, New York
April 18th, 2018

# INTRODUCTION
—

"...there are many worlds but they
            share the same sky one sky one destiny"

Kairi

Process science is the study of how energy flows through the universe. Everything I will share with you in this book ends with being able to describe the study of process science, but this isn't a book about defining or practicing a new academic discipline. This is a story about integrated discovery, learning to love, and finding purpose by understanding the universal energy pattern that governs everything in our lives.

Growing up watching TV and movies, I always thought the "meaning of life" was something to be searched for but never found. The concept was a romantic, unsolvable puzzle which the hero was meant to contemplate and answer as best he could; only to be validated by reflection at the end of his life.

I see things differently now.

The shared meaning and purpose of all our lives has been in plain sight the whole time. When I realized what it was, and how to best align with it, it brought me serenity and joy. Much of the fear I struggled with throughout my life has disappeared.

I'll admit that I ended up here by accident. It was never my intent to search for peace by understanding my place within the energy flow pattern of the universe. It was simply a consequence of my fixation with exploring the concept of process, and why the term is relevant to humans both personally and professionally.

I've always been a nag (in addition to being obsessive), and I was that proverbial kid who asked "why?" repeatedly until I was either punished or satisfied with the answer. In the context of process improvement work, which I fell into early in my career, I kept asking "why?" to many aspects of the job and kept getting back unsatisfactory answers, often creating more ambiguity than clarity. For example, if you google "process" right now, you will get back several definitions and not all are similar. In fact, the more you listen to people talk about process, the more you will notice that everyone is thinking of something different when they refer to it. Some people hate process, because to them it means bureaucracy, while others seek process because they think it will give them additional clarity or guidance within their work. If asked, most process professionals will give you a personal, as opposed to a standard, definition for the word "process".

As a young process professional, I was justifiably annoyed that I couldn't concisely define the word "process", which also meant I had no chance of clearly articulating what it meant to improve processes as a profession. To remedy this, I set out to create a standard, universal definition for process that everyone might adopt and understand. What I initially thought might be a simple exercise ended up not being solved within the week, or the next month, or even the next year. There were times when I gave up, or was distracted by other things in life, but I always had an itch associated with knowing that the clear definition of the most foundational element to process improvement was still outside of my reach. Eight years and many revelations later, I finally figured it out: process is the mechanism that transforms energy into value.

With this definition, it follows that everything is process. Anything with energy flowing through it is a process, and that includes almost everything that exists, including you. For an unknown reason, or perhaps randomly, the universe consistently seeks to create value, which is the difference between benefits and costs (value = benefit − cost); and it does so by transforming energy into value, using processes.

The way in which the universe allocates limited energy into processes is the highest order "pattern" that I will refer to in the narrative that follows. While I began to study process through the lens of business, I realized that my scope was too narrow. To come to the above definition of process, I had to integrate all my life experiences, as well as intentionally explore additional topics, including psychology, spirituality, natural science, history, and many more.

When all the knowledge I had gathered came to a critical mass, everything suddenly organized itself and I started seeing the pattern that governs processes, and the energy flowing through them. As a human process with this universal energy flowing through me, I could see myself in the pattern, and experienced such overwhelming comfort that it brought me to tears – the knowing was cathartic beyond words.

I'm going to attempt to share the knowledge I discovered, in a sequence that may help you to understand quickly what I had put together in a random way over the course of many years. I will recount events and learnings from my life that were milestones in the discovery process and put them within the context of energy flowing through three subsets of our universe: the way energy flows through nature, the way it flows through humans, and finally the way it flows through business. I hope that by sharing my personal journey you will more easily find your own process vision and can experience the same joy and calmness in better understanding the process science that governs our universe.

# NATURE'S FLOW

—

"Never does nature say one
          thing & wisdom another"

Juvenal

## VIDEO GAMES

Since childhood, I've been attracted to video games. My Dad had the first Nintendo Entertainment System, and playing it with him was the beginning of an obsession in me that has never dissipated. I didn't realize until many years later that I was developing a mind for process by spending countless hours completing the various games I had access to. Video games were my first teacher of process, and they intuitively taught me several critical pieces of the puzzle: scarcity, experimentation, and the power of simulation. The way that energy flows through nature is influenced by these same concepts, and I think many of us start to learn them through play – we just don't realize it.

If you don't know much about video games, or at least the type I enjoyed, they act as simulations of exciting, entertaining, and/or fantastical situations that we typically wouldn't be able to experience. For example, in first-person shooter (FPS) games, you play as a weapon-carrying individual who is usually forced to kill enemies in the context of a mission or dangerous situation. In role playing games (RPGs) you progress as the hero in some epic quest to save the princess, save the world, or some similar premise. No matter the context of the game, they all simulate common elements that appeal to our instincts. Simulations themselves act as a unique basis for learning, in contexts an average person normally wouldn't be able to experience. It is also a powerful learning mechanism to be able to experiment with the same simulation multiple times, each time with the ability to make different choices and observe the outcomes.

At an early age, I could see how my choices impacted situations, and if I didn't like the result, I could repeat the exercise with different variables and see how it changed my in-game fate. I later realized that simulation and iterative experimentation is the foundation of the scientific method – it's just that now, video games allow us to internalize this process from the minute we pick up and operate technology.

Access to technology and games aside, why would a child, or anyone for that matter, want to experiment with a simulation over and over again? It is because of the last element we haven't addressed yet: *scarcity*. Video games mirror the realistic energy flow through nature by setting up the construct of energy scarcity.

When you start a game, you are given a limited amount of energy to experiment with and achieve desired results. It could be currency, health points, skill points, ammunition, time, or anything else you can think of that would be useful, but it will only be provided in limited quantities. When you are in an environment with scarcity it creates urgency and pressure – this is what makes it exciting!

With limited energy, each choice during the simulation must somehow create benefits in excess of the energy it cost. That way, you can use that benefit at each subsequent stage to progressively gain more energy and move the game to completion. If you can't manage to consistently create value with your choices (energy expenditures) over time, the trials of the game will overwhelm you, resulting in starting over and trying again. Most people play games because the thrill of creating value from limited resources is viscerally satisfying, even if they don't articulate it that way. You could say that the pleasure of iteratively energizing processes that provide value is hardwired into our nature – which is exactly the case.

Scarcity of energy is the environmental condition required for benefits and value to exist as meaningful concepts. Without scarcity, there is infinity, which means that the relative energy cost of doing something (compared to the infinite amount you have of it) is always 0. If the cost in the value equation (value = benefits – cost) is always 0, it creates an interesting dynamic: value will always equal the perceived benefit, and it becomes impossible to prioritize achieving benefits that hold the same value. The inability to prioritize in this case results in random behavior when faced with a choice.

Let's take a video game example that covers scarce and infinite resource conditions:

> Resources are scarce and I have 10 energy points to make my next decision. I only need to worry about health points for the next level, and I have two food options of equal benefit to me because they provide the same amount of health points – one is meat and the other fruit. ("Benefit" as a variable in the value equation is always determined subjectively from the perspective of the agent making the value determination, which means we can quantify it however we want, knowing both benefits in question already give us the exact same thing). Let's assign the expected health point benefit an arbitrary value of 10 for this example.
>
> The last piece of information outstanding is the cost: the meat costs 8 energy points and the fruit only 3. Now we can do some math using the value equation: The meat option yields 2 value units (value (2) = benefit (10) – cost (8)), whereas the fruit option yields 7 with the same math ((value (7) = benefit (10) – cost (3)).

Intuitively, you already know you would buy the fruit, but the point is to start letting your mind relate to the value-based language that you instinctively speak without knowing it. Even though the benefit of both options is the same, the value is different considering the cost. The reason this is important should become clear when we compare it to the infinite resource scenario.

> If I have no costs in the same situation because I have infinite energy points, then the same two benefits from

our food example would also have the same value (value (10) = benefit (10)). Between two benefits with the same value, I have no way to figure out which to pick, so I would simply pick the meat or fruit at random, if I only had space for one of them. Or maybe I would grab them both if there was no restriction (why not?).

Back when I was a kid, there were in fact "cheat codes" you could enter into video games to create such conditions. Once used, you would get infinite energy resources and do whatever you wanted within the simulation's broader limitations. Not surprisingly, when these conditions were created, the drive to create value to beat the original conditions of the game disappear entirely, and the players act and entertain themselves through random activity. For me, this was a huge aha moment: the fun wasn't simply in getting to the end or having all the resources you needed, it was in the value creation itself – by discovering and putting my energy into the right choices (or processes).

Between two equal benefits with different costs, given conditions of energy scarcity, you can see that a pattern, or a "pull" is created. People will invariably conform to putting their energy where value creation is highest; value being defined by the conditions of the environment around you. It follows that over time, people will stop spending energy on benefits that yield less value than similar options, and the inferior option will eventually cease to exist. It is in this way that games also become directional, or in a way, guided. Players who buy the meat at the first stage will be punished by having less energy later, and when they replay the simulation, they will not make the same mistake considering the wasted energy on the meat. The conditions inherent to the environment force players to change the pattern in their play styles in specific ways, in order to create enough value to complete the game.

Relate this to your own experience – have you internalized some of the same dynamics of games you've played over the years (video games or otherwise)? Do you feel pulled to do certain things in your environment because it's the more efficient or effective way to do it – even if it may not be your preferred way of doing a particular thing?

Video games are simulations built in such a way that players can experiment within conditions of energy scarcity with the intent to create enough value to "win" the game. Described in this way, video games reflect the flow of energy through nature almost exactly – which in nature we call "natural selection". Even though I was only a child, playing games was the start of me internalizing the pattern of how energy is prioritized and moves through natural processes. This background helped make it easier for me to understand real life concepts when I started studying them in college.

## SCIENCE

I did my undergraduate degree at the University of Virginia, where I went with the intention to become a doctor. My degree ended up being in biology and psychology, but I also had to study the other natural sciences as part of the pre-med program.

I'll admit that I had no real reason to become a doctor. I made that decision without much thought, because in high school I was too preoccupied with video games to do any self-reflection or meaningful career planning. Despite that, the pre-med program ended up being extremely stimulating and it was there that I learned a lot of important truths that helped me to more clearly see the pattern of energy flowing through nature's processes.

Thus, science was my second process teacher, and even though I could geek out about science forever, I am going to limit this chapter to those select topics from biology, chemistry, and physics that eventually led me to major discoveries in the pattern.

Within biology, learning the theory of evolution had the most profound effect on me, as it concisely describes the processes governing nature from the beginning of life. The word *evolution* itself describes *the gradual development of something*, especially from a simple to a more complex form.

As you may remember from biology class, the scientific theory of evolution developed around the concept of *natural selection*, first articulated by Charles Darwin in 1859 in the book *On the Origin of Species*. Darwin had observed that, in nature, living things will change in small increments from generation to generation, in order to increase their ability to survive and thrive. This process of micro-evolution, which he termed natural selection, occurs as individual creatures are born with small variations in physical traits and behaviors. These variations, in turn, act as a sort of random experiment whereby those individuals whose attributes are best-optimized for survival are also most likely to reproduce and continue passing on their genes, while those with variants ill-suited to survival will not live to do so. Over time, the variants with the highest success rate of survival become the baseline and the cycle continues.

*Natural selection* – sometimes referred to as "survival of the fittest" – distills all the complexity we see in nature to a simple, verifiable pattern of genetic inheritance that reacts to the changing conditions of scarce energy resources in the environment. Just like in my childhood video games, scarcity of resources is what fundamentally drives process prioritization for living organisms. Those animals that represented the most effective process to transform scarce energy into benefits were selected over others to survive and build flow and direction within the pattern.

Darwin's theories have taught me more about process than any other single source of knowledge, and there's not a day that goes by where I don't see the pattern in nature unfolding around me as consistently as he observed it in the 19th century. While I would encourage everyone to further reflect on *On the Origin of Species*, I will move on for now to my own critical learnings from evolutionary theory which are necessary for the conversation at hand.

Within *phylogenetics*, or the study of evolutionary histories of organisms, there exists a concept called "maximum parsimony". I'll never forget the day I learned this, because it represents a paradox from our perspective. It states that when studying the complexity of changes that an organism could have undergone during its evolutionary history, the smallest amount of changes that cohesively ties the evolutionary history together is acknowledged as most accurately representing the correct path through time.

This helped me understand the relativity of natural "complexity", and that randomness for the sake of being complicated is rarely exhibited in nature. The energy that flows through nature manifests itself through highly complex details from the human perspective, but it navigates that complexity in a very ordered and surprisingly simple manner.

From nature's perspective, nothing is complicated, but is simply the path of least resistance to evolve and continue the creation of value from its own perspective. It's a basic pattern, and one that is starting to resonate more with humans as they seek structures that are more "organic".

*Organic*, in the context of human invention, refers to *structures that are more like living organisms* as opposed to the linear, simplistic structures that have represented human design since the industrial revolution. New Age thinkers are starting to understand that the perceived complexity in natural structures may appear random or indecipherable, but there is incredible value and efficiency in its form, sometimes beyond our comprehension.

This acknowledgement, that we as humans can trust the simple pattern of organic optimization which lies behind all the complexity that nature represents, is moving us towards what I consider to be the next level of understanding evolutionary theory. I acquired an affinity for "organic" structures more intuitively than some, as studying evolution established in me an incredible respect and deference for nature that many don't adopt as zealously.

When you contemplate the logic of natural selection, it stands to reason that everything that presently exists is close to the best it can be at producing value in its given environment.

It's never a question about whether something makes sense, it's a question about how it makes sense.

I see a lot of people who have lost this truth, in the arrogance that is associated with human ingenuity. People think of nature as aimless or simple in purpose, not equipped to create beauty and form like only the human mind can conceive. We sought to improve on nature by mechanizing and automating the very limited aspects that we could understand over the last few hundred years, in hindsight often to negative results (e.g. monocropping). This notion that there is strength inherent to natural models boils down to a simple mantra that has brought me great success in applying process improvement over the years: *if a process exists, there is value being produced.*

Practically speaking, you should always seek to understand what exists in front of you before attempting to change or improve it. If there was no value being produced by something, then it wouldn't exist for you to observe or study!

Think back to the pattern of energy flow we started to establish in the video game discussion. Energy stops flowing through processes that don't transform that energy into value. Unless you're observing something in transition, the living processes in nature won't exist for long if they don't produce value. Just as games establish direction in the processes they want players to use in order to navigate the simulated environment, nature is structured the same way; except that in nature the environment is our world, and the player is the universe deciding how to channel energy through nature, and by extension, through us. This is the most significant addition to what Darwin started to articulate with his theory of natural selection: to say that the universe has direction, driven by its own definition of "benefit," and its own assignment of value to certain processes over others.

What is the benefit I'm alluding to? What does the universe value? Which processes does the universe prefer over others? The answer to these questions eluded me for a long time. In some ways I was confused because of the narrow geological timeline in which Darwin studied living forms, and the reverence I had for the absolute logic of natural selection. In Darwin's view, things got stronger and more complex simply as a matter of mutating and being randomly better at surviving in the face of dynamic environmental conditions.

While this might be comprehensive if you set your scope of observation from the beginning of life, the universe didn't start with life; it started with nothing but inanimate energy; so Darwin's pattern wasn't complete. Why would living things be driven to survive in the first place? Why does everything with form strive to maintain its physical form? From the beginning, there was no such thing as survival, because nothing was alive. Yet the universe's energy selectively flowed into processes nonetheless.

The pattern of what was produced by processes over the entire history of the universe tells us empirically the universe's definition of value: the transformation of energy into increasingly complex physical forms. This is also the purpose of all life, a purpose shared by every process in the universe. Nature is a collection of living processes that receive energy from the universe in the same way it has been distributed since the start of form.

Everything that exists and lives strives to create more complex patterns of form. It is what the pattern defined by the universe created us to do.

The actual origin of the universe is irrelevant to our conversation, but–for the sake of narrative–I'll borrow what I understand from Stephen Hawking's *A Brief History of Time*, and assume that the universe suddenly burst from nothing into physical form with a giant explosion that scattered basic particles throughout the universe. These first particles (or some basic combination of them) are what I refer to when I talk about "energy". They were particles with the potential to create motion (e.g., more complex form), and ultimately life. In addition to exploding itself into existence, it did so with scarce, finite energy. The origin of our universe is almost magic as far as we understand it, and it could have been just as plausible that the universe created itself with an infinite source of energy to power it – but it didn't.

My point here is that as soon as the universe began, it created a dynamic of energy scarcity, which is the foundation for a value-based process prioritization system to exist. In the simplest sense, after energy brought itself into existence it began to bind together through process to create value, evolving through increasingly complex forms. Energy became dust, dust became rocks, rocks became planets, and other particles combined to become other more advanced celestial bodies with their own properties, like our sun and moon. Whichever way you look at it, it is a pattern that only goes one way: in aggregate, process never takes energy and reduces the complexity of forms over time. It is self-driving and directional. It is not the result of random scientific events, but is the direction of the universe itself, playing out consistently over time.

From the Law of Conservation of Energy, we know that energy can never be created or destroyed, it only changes form. All forms that have been created, from rocks to galaxies to humans, are made up of the same fundamental units of energy taking on increasingly complex forms driven by the universe's selective flow of energy into some processes over others. In the universe's pattern of creating increasingly complex form, life and nature were created.

From Earth's perspective, when the first self-replicating proteins became animated, life began, and the universe had established a game, a living simulation, to create more complex forms at an exponentially faster rate than ever before. This brings the origin story back to where we started this chapter: the study of natural sciences.

Science has revealed a lot of the process story, and I'll end this chapter with my greatest learning from chemistry. Before you understand chemistry, when you look at a glass of water, you see water. You see that it's a bluish liquid, and you learn that you can drink it to support your bodily processes.

Once you learn chemistry you know, despite what your eyes see, that what you are actually looking at is an unfathomable amount of hydrogen and oxygen atoms interacting with each other at a rate and scale which is also beyond your comprehension. It is a living latticework of energy binding together inanimate atoms, constantly changing form based on what it needs to do to create value. Once you have this knowledge, you can begin to think beyond your senses, and realize to a large extent that your standard view of the universe is unique to you as a human, boxed in by the limits of your own physiology.

This is the concept of 'umwelt, or the "self-centered world", a term drawn from the field of semiotics and first used by the scientist Jakob von Uexküll. My deepest hope with this book is to expand your process vision, or your ability to see the flow of energy, beyond your umwelt by making you aware of the universal patterns that exist beyond your physical senses. You won't physically see anything differently the more you know; however, you will understand everything in a fundamentally different way. You will be seeing beyond your umwelt, and that type of vision sits within your consciousness.

## WATER

*Science gives us the background to better understand and see the true nature of our universe, but it is flow that allows us to see the movement through it.*

After college, I decided not to go into medicine and had a bit of a post-grad crisis. I worked a few random jobs for a while including waiting tables at Outback Steakhouse, serving as a salesperson for Abercrombie & Fitch, and selling insurance policies on the street.

After I admitted to myself that I wasn't cut out to sell insurance, I was able to leverage my UVA degree to network into what I considered my first real job: a pilot plant engineer at a water and wastewater treatment equipment engineering company. They usually hired civil or mechanical engineers, but a decent interview, coupled with my biology and chemistry background, landed me the role. The company sold large scale water treatment technologies; our typical clients were cities or municipalities. These technologies would be giant filter units, or bioreactors, able to clean millions of gallons of water per day.

As part of the sales team, I managed the small-scale pilot units when we were called upon to test our technology against competitors, with the intent to prove in a pilot study that our technology was the best option from an effectiveness and cost standpoint. For a given study, I was responsible for building the smaller pilot unit ('smaller' being the size of a large truck and capable of processing hundreds of gallons of water per minute), getting it to the client site, and running the study using the client's water at their location. I did this job for about two years, and in the process I spent a tremendous amount of time with my third teacher of process: water.

I spent those two years at the water treatment company thinking and learning a lot about water, and nonetheless I never felt like I was even close to understanding its complexity. Water is a complicated and cruel master. Because the properties of water in a natural environment are so complex, I had to leverage all my paltry undergraduate knowledge of biology, chemistry, and physics so as not to embarrass myself on job sites.

When you pull water out of a river (or worse, the sewage line) it is filled with life and energy. From microorganisms, to plants, to small animals, all manner of things make their lives in water. Beyond that, there are huge amounts of mixed organic and inorganic solids, metals, complex human waste, and other minerals and trace chemicals. Then there is the energy itself, which moves in water and manifests in the form of heat, kinetic, or chemical energy. And on top of all those variables… water flows.

Flow was the most difficult part of managing water, because it's always on the move. Flow represents directional, continuous, uninterrupted motion. Water is the quintessential example of flow, and spending the better part of two years in a trailer watching it move got me very well acquainted with the principles of flow.

What was I doing in that trailer the whole time? I was dumping chemicals into flowing water in order to treat it. I was wrestling with my pilot machine configuration to speed up or slow down the flow through the unit, attempting to manage contact time and kinetic energy. I was also testing different combinations of chemicals, dosage, and energy combinations, followed by monitoring and sampling the results. All these activities were done to meet our water treatment objectives and create a defensible report that highlighted the strengths of the technology and various chemical configurations.

During this work, I not only came to respect the power of flow, but also to understand the consequences of impeding or creating obstacles to flow. Water flows for a lot of reasons, but unless you're wasting a ton of energy pumping it and making it flow yourself, most water treatment plants try to capture the natural flow of water based on gravity and the movement of the Earth. That source of flow (gravity) is very powerful, especially with large bodies of flowing water. Blocking that flow can be very difficult.

The one thing I internalized very strongly from this experience is that to block flow, you need to be ready to spend energy to counter the existing energy coming at you. Flow has direction, power, and is already moving. To go against it means to expend energy in the opposite direction. You already know the answer to the question "would you rather swim upstream or downstream in a flowing river in order to move yourself?" This is an important process principle: *it costs energy to create mechanisms that block flow.*

The other important lesson I learned here is that unless you block flow completely, it will continue to push forward, shatter any obstacles you place in its path, or otherwise find ways to get around your barriers. Water is notoriously brutal in this way. If you plan to change or impede flowing water, you'd better have a, well, "water-tight" solution; otherwise, be ready for the water to figure out how to get around the blockage and continue on its way.

The principles I learned about water made it easier for me to see the pattern in energy flow more broadly. Energy flow behaves the exact same way as flowing water – if something flows, it has direction, power, and intent, inherent to its behavior. An intuitive example of the universe's flow of energy into nature is the constant flow of photons from the Sun to the Earth. You can even imagine this as a perpetual river of energy that pours forth from the Sun into all processes on our planet.

In the case of the universe, instead of gravity being the source of flow, the source is the behavioral pattern of the universe itself as exhibited by its choice to concentrate energy into processes that create more value through complex form. Whichever processes create more value, these attract more energy to themselves over time, thus creating the pull, or the flow. The flow of energy from the universe is incomprehensible in power and magnitude.

Like water, if you set up obstacles that act against this energetic flow, it immediately finds ways to flow around them, and in time it will always destroy those obstacles.

The rest of nature is more aware of the flow than we humans are, and doesn't set up obstacles or purposely block that energy flow. Generally, non-human life exhibits a synergy with the universe that we as humans have not been locked into. We have the free will to set up barriers or go against that flow at our own discretion. It was never the universe's intent for us to do this, but it is a natural byproduct of the flexibility and power we were given. It is in this way that the flow of energy through nature differs significantly from the flow of energy through humans.

## ONENESS

While we have spent some time establishing a foundation of definitions related to process science, this last chapter will deliver what the section title promised: the patterns of energy flow through the collection of living processes that represent nature.

This flow is the simplest pattern, following the general theme that nature seems complex, but actually operates via a small number of fixed principles. The reason for this simplicity in flow is that nature is truly one with the universe, separate only in that it is an extension of the universe that is "alive" from our perspective. That oneness means that there is never any difference between what the universe wants and what nature is doing.

For most of my childhood, my dad was the parent who stayed home with the kids while my mom worked. He is a very active man and loved taking me and my sisters into Washington D.C. for day-long trips to visit parks, museums, and the national zoo.

I have a lot of fond memories of spending the day at the zoo, and–for a child with a notoriously short attention span–I would be entranced for hours watching animals and running around the different exhibits. One of my sharper memories from those days involves seeing the ant colony exhibit for the first time – the type where you see the entire colony working in their chambers through a see-through pane of glass. A zoo staff member pointed out where the queen was and explained the different classes of ants, as well as how they all had their own function to support the colony. You could see the speckles of green plant matter along the black rivers of ants constantly moving back and forth from the nurseries and other important functional areas of ant life. It was the first time I registered the "hive mind" structure of life, and it always fascinated me that disparate living things could work so synchronously to promote the same agenda – the ants are all separate, but in terms of energy and purpose, they are one.

I'm not the only one who thinks this concept is cool. The *hive mind* construct shows up a lot in fantasy and sci-fi; some of my favorite examples include the bug race from *Ender's Game* by Orson Scott Card, the Borg race from the Star Trek series, and the Zerg race from StarCraft.

The idea of the *hive mind* is that a species is organized by being differentiated functionally and yet collectively represents a single entity, as opposed to being a collection of multi-functional individuals each attempting to survive on their own (e.g. mammals). There is usually a "queen bee" or some central heart or brain to the species, and all the other organisms are in service to that higher-level organism. It's not that different conceptually from the way the cells in your body all act in concert to collectively form "you". If I transformed "you" into a hive mind-type organism, it would be as if your head and brain got to relax in a safe space at home while your limbs leave the house and autonomously heed your will to gather food and make money and return these resources to you.

The relationship between the universe and nature is very similar to the one between a hive brain and its various subordinate organisms. The energy pattern of a hive can be seen as uninterrupted signals coordinating everyone in concert with the brain's will. In the case of the universe, it similarly coordinates all its inanimate and animate parts as instruments to more effectively fulfill its pattern in creating more complex forms. Just as the ant queen spends her energy to spawn worker ants, which then devote their entire lifecycle without question to her bidding, nature is similarly subject to the universe.

The combination of organic and inorganic components greatly enhanced the universe's ability to iterate form, and for millions of years it enjoyed the ability to supply a continuous energy flow to nature and be rewarded with the emergence of increasingly complex and beautiful forms. If you imagine that nature in its entirety is a single extension (a worker ant) of the universe (the queen ant), it will be easier to conceptualize that the energy flow through it is always balanced and even – it does not set up obstacles to its own flow or resist its master's will. By separating species that could only breed with each other, the universe set up discrete variables and functions that could evolve on their own paths and co-exist to form ecosystems that flexibly balanced themselves within a dynamic, inorganic universe.

For form to continue to evolve in complexity, it had to build more complex species in stages, each setting up stability in the ecosystem to support more complex forms. For example, if plants hadn't come first, things that eat plants couldn't have come after them.

Also, nature would have faced a problem if these plants tried to replace themselves altogether with plant-eating animals, because then those animals would have had nothing to eat. If you think about it in terms of the pattern, nature stabilized the value production of a species, and as a result, species with more complex form were able to discreetly introduce themselves into the system, and a beautiful ecosystem continued to evolve co-dependently.

Let's think of nature more simply as a collection of different species that interact in a shared environment. The species level could be considered the basic unit of experimentation from the universe's perspective. Each species represent a single, unique process. They take only certain energy inputs and produce value in a way that only that particular species can do.

Despite the uniqueness of conditions and value creation for every species, they all play by the same rules and collectively represent one entity. Species don't kill more than they can eat, acquire or hoard resources they can't use, or endanger themselves needlessly for emotional reasons – they live in balance with an absolute knowledge of the universe's pattern. They consistently and cautiously survive, and when they reach evolutionary stability within the current environment, a new natural function can evolve–in the form of a new species.

From our perspective as humans, it is hard for us to relate to the hive mind, or the oneness, that synchronizes species or animals together without strong individual identity. For me, it became easier to grasp by reflecting on the human construct of "time", and the impact of nature not recognizing such a concept.

Humans think of everything in terms of time. However, it's actually an arbitrary measurement construct that doesn't represent anything physical. If you put yourself in the universe's perspective where there is only physical form, time and other intellectual constructs don't exist.

An example would be the human measurement construct of a meter. A meter describes an amount of something, but a meter itself doesn't exist. It's a metaphysical language construct to help us relate to an amount of physical existence (i.e. a meter stick) more quickly than if we described the amount to someone by using an alternative approach. When I say the universe doesn't recognize things that don't exist, it is because it has no need to relate things to other things, like we do. To the universe, everything simply is as it is.

Time is the same type of construct as distance, and generally speaking, what it helps us measure is changes in form. Personally, I struggled with this for a long time (sometimes to the point of self-described insanity), and I still can't explain it to you in words, because every word in the human language is bound by a time orientation (explaining when and where things are in time relative to each other).

For example, even words like "measure" and "change", which I just used in my loose definition, are bound in time, implying states of being before and after each other. We're not going to spend a lot of time here because it is a vexing conversation to have, but I recommend you internalize it as truth that time doesn't exist, and from this point, let your brain work on what that means in the background of your consciousness. It is important to acknowledge here, because understanding the absence of time is foundational to understanding the pattern.

I can "see" the existence of form without time, but it can only construct itself as energy patterns and images in my mind's eye, because again, this understanding can't be articulated within our current language constraints. (If you wish to gain a better grasp of this topic, I recommend first studying an abbreviated version of Einstein's work on the relativity of time, which helped my brain process this concept when I first started contemplating it.)

Nature is a direct extension of the universe's intelligence; so, by extension, it cannot recognize time. Because of this, nature can only operate in the present moment. Without being able to conceive a future or a past, nature can't possibly act selfishly, emotionally, or irrationally, because its full attention is always focused on what's happening in that very moment.

Not being able to think in time also means that animals can't perceive scarcity. The universe (the brain, the thinker) operates and prioritizes energy flow based on scarcity, but nature does not. If you perpetually live in the moment, there is only what is around you, so the concept of things "running out" can't be considered – you either have something right now or you don't. Not comprehending scarcity also means that animals can't be afraid in the same way we are. They can *seem* afraid, and they certainly avoid danger and death, but fear as humans experience it comes from the unknown – animals always know everything they need to know because it's happening right then. This is the major reason why animals always seem at peace, and that connecting with them allows us to share that sense of peace. It is because the energy flow through nature is without fear.

This is important to relate back to the idea that *evolving directionally is based on prioritizing choices with a consistent progression*. Nature does not have the same flexibility or ability to make choices for where its energy goes; the energy it receives is more in the form of a directive from the universe, like when we use our brains to send energy to our limbs.

I got my first dog in college and have had dogs ever since. When I observe them, my first impulse, right or wrong, is to personify them and relate to them within the context of my human psyche. Can dogs love and recognize you, and all these things? Yes, definitely – but it's different from how we do with each other. The way a dog processes the world is always in the present moment; and everything they do is with intent, based on instinct and given whatever circumstance is going on right then.

Whether it's sleeping, or cuddling, or begging, or playing, the dog is responding instinctively to its environment in order to improve its biological fitness. Dogs are like very complicated machines with one program: keep your process alive so that it can continue to fulfill its unique value proposition. For domesticated house pets and other animals that support human form, it is in supporting our energy flow that they have departed from their own. Even with that being the case, however, their behavior is still consistent with their stable evolutionary position in nature.

As a living process, animals only have one mode: on, and it never deviates from its design of a) processing what's going on in its environment, b) creating value through stabilizing the ecosystem, and c) contributing to more complex form. This has a lot of implications which you can verify through observing natural behavior, but generally it allows us to think of each species as a single process that will only ever do one thing within the physiological boundaries set by the system – like differentiated hive functions.

It is because it is so predictable and reliable that our ecosystem has been able to grow so diverse and complex. Without the stability of nature's pattern, chaos would have prevented complex form from getting to this iteration in the first place. Imagine if every ant in the colony had its own will and could behave in its own interest without considering the colony's survival. The chance of the queen meeting her objective to survive and propagate the colony would be severely diminished by the random behavior of individual worker ants.

The universe has only two types of energy flow through nature: doing and changing, which it balances based on the dynamics we have been discussing in order to most efficiently meet its goals. When I say two types of energy flow, you can think of it as nature being organized into two types of processes, and these processes form the only channels where the universe invests energy.

The constantly activated "on" mode of nature I casually referenced earlier is the "doing" process type of energy transformation, and represents one flow path. This is the state of transforming energy directly into value by changing the physical environment in ways that stabilize a living process' ability to stay alive (or more simply for an animal, converting energy into the act of living).

The other flow path for energy is the "changing" process type, which represents energy being transformed into variation as a mechanism to experiment and iteratively navigate the environment, in order to make sure that the "doing" process stays relevant and continues propagating form. Energy flowing through changing processes manifests itself as all the mechanisms that promote genetic mutation and diversity in organisms. The doing versus changing mechanic will appear in different contexts as we progress to the discussion about energy flow through humans and business, but fundamentally, the universe only prioritizes energy on those two process paths.

In nature, these two energy flows always occur simultaneously at the species level. An individual animal can only ever be doing things; however, at the species level, energy is spent in changing at the same time, through mutation and variation within the species itself. Let's say my dog has a litter of 6 puppies. Each puppy individually will only perpetually do things based on its form and process design, but each puppy will be slightly different. This is the universe's way of experimenting and iterating within the simulation. Some of that energy will go into puppies that are inferior, given present environmental circumstances. That energy will end up going to waste, to a certain extent, as that puppy's genes fall out of the gene pool.

Energy spent in changing processes is always going to yield less value compared to energy spent in doing processes. That cost is offset by the puppies that end up stronger or more fit than the parents. When they proceed to do what they are meant to do, their form will continue to become more stable in the environment, produce more value, and support the continuation of the pattern. The value that offsets the opportunity cost of the changing flow is that it acts like insurance that reduces risk and ensures the system of natural form remains viable. This is a different way to describe and expand on evolutionary mechanics, with increased attention to the way in which the universal flow of energy is prioritized through nature.

This worked well for the universe for a very long time, but the pattern is always changing to produce more value. How does the universe know when it should change the pattern to create increasingly more value? With nature working well, why ever change the pattern?

The answer lies in the fixed aspects of nature's process. The ability for nature to gain more complexity in form has a maximum energy to value transformation rate: a species can only change form through natural selection, limited by certain physiological barriers to dramatic mutation, and new forms can only emerge with ecosystem stability.

Am I suggesting the universe is impatient and wants to evolve faster? Not exactly. We have now acknowledged the fact that from the universe's perspective—and nature's as a subset of the universe—time doesn't exist. It's not about moving faster or slower, but rather, it's about the pattern in energy flow becoming more efficient, focused, and higher in magnitude. Remember that the flow of energy is constantly favoring process that produces more value. As energy flow continues to favor certain processes over others, those processes have more intense flow. If, like most processes we observe, the transformation of energy flow into value doesn't scale 1:1, plateaus eventually occur which result in large build ups and resistance to the increased flow.

Imagine the universe's favorite process as a very large pipe. At first, while flow is finding that pipe, energy flows straight through and value is created as fast as the flow itself. As the magnitude of flow increases, the physical structure of the pipe itself eventually becomes its own barrier, and energy flow becomes constricted (like pushing more water faster through a fixed pipe).

Just as in chemistry, when energy builds up at a certain configuration, it allows for dramatic transition states to be navigated and more efficient and complex forms to emerge. From my perspective, these events in the history of the universe are few, and we've already covered one: the emergence of life and nature. Initially, the universe spent a long time optimizing energy flow to create complex, inanimate forms. After the inanimate universe became stable, energy density in the overall process reached a critical mass. At this point, flow started to become impeded or blocked by the system itself. At this juncture, life emerged, and again the flow started to become more efficient by routing energy to a new pipe (organic life).

What happened when the energy flowing through nature and living creatures couldn't keep up with the stronger flow and again hit a new milestone?

Us. Humans emerged.

All the value and complexity that nature created led up to the milestone of our creation as a new species, in order to more efficiently continue the pattern. As humans we are strongly tied to the flow of energy through nature, but also have new process mechanisms to manage and control that flow at an individual level, unlike our animal counterparts. While nature can only do and change at the species level, humans were given the ability to process doing and changing energy types at the species and individual level.

The ability to harness the energy for changing at the individual level has untethered human evolution from generation to generation iteration, substantially speeding up the human ability to adapt and propagate form. Individual humans can iterate and evolve alongside their broader species' evolution.

This milestone of humanity is as significant to the pattern as the emergence of life itself when the universe was only inanimate energy. As a part of nature, humans are still subject to the universe's pattern to create more complex form. It is our purpose, and what all energy flow we receive is meant to do, but we have more powerful and flexible ways to achieve that purpose than anything that existed before us.

In the next section, we'll discuss how human processes build upon the doing and changing energy flow pattern, in a way that allows more flow to move through us compared to all of nature combined.

# HUMAN FLOW

—

"One of the first conditions of happiness
	is that the link between man & nature
		shall not be broken"

Leo Tolstoy

## THINKING

I find it amusing to imagine watching the universe's pattern unfold from the beginning of time as if it were a movie.

As I watch this movie in my head, we've reached the point in the narrative where the next huge milestone event is about to explode into being, as the energy flow density through nature starts reaching a critical mass.

Suddenly, the event occurs, and then we're all shocked and confused by the seemingly anticlimactic arrival of the human baby. This summation of all nature's power manifests itself as a useless, fragile, fleshy lump of a thing, with no claws, fangs, wings, or physical advantage of any kind. Not only is it like a rather clumsy larva, with nothing to do but eat and wiggle around, it also stays that way for an incredibly long time – it's almost a year before it becomes serviceably ambulatory and it certainly can't take care of itself for a long while after that.

What special ability could this pathetic creature possibly possess, to justify giving up almost every other survival advantage that nature had iterated towards since the beginning of life? You already know the punchline, what the universe is so proud of: *humans possess the ability to think.*

Humans are part of nature and are therefore subject to the incredible strength and density of energy flowing through the already-established doing and changing processes in that part of the pattern. As an animal species, we are driven to stabilize our ecosystem and constantly propagate form, as well as to experience the change and variation between individuals that make us all unique and uniquely fit for different contexts.

The pattern-expanding capability that humanity evolved was *the at-will ability to step out of nature's energy flow and route some of that energy flow to uniquely human processes.*

These new process elements allow us to change ourselves by creating and integrating new processes into our form throughout our individual lifetime. This is the function of thinking.

*Thinking* is *the human flow version of the changing process in nature,* and when we commit energy to thinking, we can contemplate how to evolve by our own will. Animals can't decide how or when to evolve, they only ever transform energy through doing processes. Change just happens to them over generations because of the changing processes built into the universe's pattern. In this light, humans' ability to control energy through changing processes is the first instance where some decision-making power over the creation of form was exhibited within a living organism.

In the pattern, this created an interesting dynamic: *humans are the transition between nature and a smaller version of the universe itself.* Being undifferentiated but adaptable at birth makes sense, in the context of us being able to decide our own evolutionary path throughout our life cycle. We are all part of a species, but also individually each represent our own species in that we have the power to do and change within a single form.

The miraculous tool we gained to do this is what we call consciousness. I'm not going to spend any more time discussing my perspective on consciousness, but I would recommend some self-study (e.g. *Waking Up* by Sam Harris) so that you can feel more comfortable about what exactly this thing is that enables us to think. However you want to conceptualize it in your mind, I'm now going to explain the implications of consciousness in terms of the pattern, and how using thinking to step out of nature's flow into a uniquely human flow is both incredibly empowering and, counterintuitively, very dangerous.

What do I mean, exactly, when I say that we can "step out of nature's flow"?

When we talk about the doing and changing processes happening simultaneously in nature, this is possible because nature is guiding the doing energy, and the pattern itself automatically guides the changing energy. To be doing both simultaneously means that the flow of nature is designed for constant action. To be fully aligned in nature's flow as a human, you would constantly be in a state of doing and contributing to the creation of new form and would have no time for thinking or changing (i.e. you would be like all the other animals).

For humans, stepping out of this flow is exactly that: when you engage your power to think, your consciousness separates you at that moment from the flow of energy through nature and your physical form, and you can temporarily stop some of your doing processes and begin changing (or thinking) processes. It is in this way that we are more evolved than our animal counterparts; animals can't modify their behavior beyond what they personally experience, and even that modification is a matter of instinct versus conscious choice. But most of us can only exist predominantly in one state at a time – our consciousness is both the key and the gateway which allows us to switch modes.

When we step into the place of thinking through our consciousness, we transport part of ourselves into a metaphysical thinking realm where we have direct access to a different kind of knowledge and energy reserved for the processes of change. It is in this place where we almost immediately become aware of scarcity, along with all the dynamics it creates, which is prerequisite to having the power to prioritize processes that transform energy into change.

In this "thinking realm," there are many things we can do with our energy. Think of it as a large cosmic space to which we can teleport and execute thinking processes. Energy spent in thinking should be reserved for experimentation, with the intent to use the results to evolve your form – the same way that the changing energy that comes directly from the universe enacts change in nature.

Changing processes are not as efficient at creating value as doing processes, so any energy which you spend in the thinking realm is inherently less productive. Thinking processes are meant to help us extract value from experiences that we don't have to physically experience (sort of like video games); this is a very efficient mechanism to inform decisions in how to evolve your form.

Examples of activities we can engage in within the thinking realm would include, but are not limited to, empathizing with others as a means of gaining experience, simulating possible experiences, learning directly from distilled experience, or integrating knowledge from multiple experiences. Basically, the thinking realm is where we can live thousands of lives' worth of simulated experiences (from anything's perspective), and then bring that knowledge back into our physical form within nature's flow, in order to add to our natural processes in the pursuit of creating more complex form.

At this point you might be skeptical about the idea that thinking teleports a part of you to another dimension to experience things. I'll now challenge you to validate the notion by stepping out of your body for a moment and imagining what it would be like to look at yourself when you're deep in thought.

What are you physically doing at that moment? The answer is some form of nothing, or automated behavior. When you catch yourself distracted by thought, zoom out and imagine how an outsider would describe you in that moment. Staring into nothing, standing still and oblivious to what's around you, distracted and making obvious mistakes doing whatever you're trying to do. Do these descriptions sound familiar at all?

Where are you at that moment when you become a partial zombie and bungle around in the real world? If we zoom out even further and look at society, we are all going through our day, coming in and out of nature's flow whenever we take time to engage our consciousness and think. It is a parade of people starting and pausing throughout the day, their consciousness jerking in and out of the physical plane. If you imagine your body as a car, and your consciousness as the passenger, it would be like stopping the car and stepping out for a break every few minutes on the way to your destination.

This is really what it means to step in and out of nature's flow, and we're so used to it within society we don't even pause to appreciate how erratic (especially compared to other animals) it makes our physical behavior. I personally feel this most strongly when I'm lying in bed wrestling with thinking before sleep. In the physical world I'm lying there like a vegetable, an empty vessel waiting for its consciousness to return. I compare this to Kingsley, my dog, who is usually sleeping a few feet from me, and who is always alert and present, even in sleep. It is in these moments of awareness when I try hardest not to return to the thinking realm and let my body ease into slumber.

Speaking of Kingsley, have you ever tried to surprise a dog? Surprising humans is easy because we're all half-empty vessels most of the time wandering around on autopilot. Catching animals by surprise is much more difficult because they're always fully in their physical form, filtering inputs from the environment into appropriate action. Sometimes when Kingsley appears to be in a deep sleep, I'll suppress my presence as much as possible and slowly approach him with the intent to startle him. Incredibly, most of the time he still senses me coming and barely reacts beyond a slight jerk when I shout or pounce on him.

There was one time that remains sharp in my memory, where I successfully caught him off guard and I got the reaction I was looking for. When his fight or flight instinct activated he pulled his upper lip back in a snarl, his eyes dilated, and any recognition of our relationship was non-existent. In that next fraction of a second, I thought he would bite or otherwise defend himself against me. I was frozen in time while I processed the error I might have just made, but in the same instant he recognized me, and his entire body reconfigured back into calmness.

What is so interesting is that in that moment, I didn't get any reflection of fear in his energy – he was simply reacting appropriately to what might have been a serious threat to his form, and then immediately reverted into his placid normal state of being after instantly processing the situation. I'm sharing this story because the power of being fully present never ceases to amaze me. For me, this interaction serves as a reminder of what we often give up unknowingly by letting our consciousness linger too long in the thinking realm.

In reality, moving in and out of nature's flow is not binary, meaning you can never fully leave it; nor can we, as humans, ever be 100% in nature's flow either – we're not built that way. Like many things, the balance of where you are channeling the energy flowing through you is on a continuum. Animals have no choice but to be 100% in nature's flow; but for us, we have been given control, to some extent, over how the foundational doing and changing energy we get from the universe can be harnessed for human-specific processes.

There are certain aspects of our physical form that can never leave nature's flow, such as some of our autonomous body systems, the ones that keep us alive by breathing, telling us that we're hungry or thirsty, circulating our blood, etc. These core "doing" process elements that link us to nature keep us rooted, and give us a place to always re-orient our energy flow. This is why, when we wish to return to the present moment, we are often advised to bring our attention to our breath. This rootedness in the involuntary doing processes which sustain our life functions also allows us to enter the thinking realm fluidly while our bodies still perform basic tasks that are automated—such as walking around or doing rather "mindless" activity.

Imagine if we could move our energy 100% out of nature's flow. If that was the case, even accidentally, we would imagine it as our body suddenly slumping over and our consciousness drifting back into the thinking realm with no way to return to our body. This might be what you would experience in a perpetual dream state, like sleeping at night, a coma, or death – it's hard to say. In any case, we don't have to worry about that because we're anchored to the flow of energy through nature by design. Our total form is meant to have control over the balance throughout our life, so that we can evolve in a way that no other living thing can.

I imagine it as though the main pipe that represents our processes has extra controls. It is always filled with energy from nature's flow, but we have a control valve that leads to a smaller pipe where we can route an amount of our nature energy into a flow unique to human processes. Consciousness is the control valve, and all the incredible value that only humans can provide is made possible by the value transforming through that "human-only" energy pipe.

I had a profound realization about the power of thinking and simulation after attending a Yale lecture from Dr. Paul Bloom, the author of *Against Empathy, the Case for Rational Compassion*, who is well-known for articulating the dangers of empathetic thinking. He first spoke to something I had already intuited: using the power of empathy to simulate somebody's misfortune (such as simulating the feelings of a starving child in a developing country) offers little value to you, and in fact can be misleading when you bring the product of that thinking back to your body and let it manifest as ungrounded, irrational worry, and fear. The over saturation of negative, painful, violent, and emotionally evocative media is specifically designed to extort your ability to empathize with situations outside of your control as a means to stimulate or influence you. If you let these emotional manifestations change your course of action, you are now evidencing signs of irrationality and madness.

This notion made sense, but what caught me off guard was when he shifted into the positive use of empathy. He asserted that empathy could be used for good when simulating situations of heroism or virtue and extracting the reasoning behind why the hero made the choices he made.

We are not often placed in situations in our daily lives where we must make a choice of great self-sacrifice or heroism, but we can empathize with heroes from fantasy and fictional works that do. The ability to simulate ourselves as the hero placed in challenging situations gives us the power to learn positively from a difficult experience that we will most likely never face. It allows us to contemplate the reasons why certain decisions of great importance should be made one way versus another. We can then internalize that learning and apply it to less intense, similar situations as they arise.

I had never contemplated empathy that way, and this thought led me to better understand the duality behind the mechanics that make thinking such a powerful force behind human evolution. Empathy is one of many double-edged swords available to us in the thinking realm that can be used negatively in wasteful simulation or positively in the pursuit of knowledge.

With the knowledge of scarcity comes the power to discern value and create incredible things, but it also brings the immediate awareness of our own mortality and all the ambiguity, helplessness, and fear that comes with it. When you first visit the thinking realm at a certain maturity level, your consciousness automatically creates time to measure the scarcity of your physical form. With time comes the constructs of past and future, imaginary structures used to simulate and empathize with situations we are not presently experiencing in the physical world.

It is common to fall into the habit of making judgements about how your reality in physical space should have turned out in the past - or should turn out in the future. These judgements cause expectations which can distort reality in the physical world if you let your consciousness bring them back with you, out of the thinking realm. Any simulations run carelessly, resulting in subjective, incomplete information, or physical triggers of instinctual chemical body responses (emotion), are distracting to bring back to the real world from the thinking realm.

Imagine you are a pearl diver and your days are spent on a boat in a beautiful tropical locale. The peace you find enjoying the weather and resting between dives is the peace of being in nature, and knowing that you are in the process of being productive. Diving in the water to find pearls is like moving into the thinking realm, except instead of pearls, you seek objective knowledge derived from the universe itself.

We are not made to linger too long in the water; we are meant to go in cautiously and return to the boat with the pearls we discover there. To stay in the water too long, or to bring things back up with us that are not pearls, are paths to frustration and unhappiness, or the worst case, drowning. The only purpose to thinking is to find objective knowledge that is most relevant to you, and quickly return to ourselves so that we can integrate that knowledge into more productive forms of doing. Knowledge employed this way, into new forms of human doing, become processes in the "knowing" energy flow.

## KNOWING

*Knowing processes* are the partner to thinking processes. This is what we channel part of nature's doing energy into, for human endeavors. As you start to build the pattern in your mind, you can see the parallel of nature's doing and changing to human knowing and thinking.

*Knowing is the primary energy flow in which to put your knowledge gained by thinking into action.* When you are out of the thinking realm, you are using energy to do two types of processes. The basic doing processes are the same as those of other animals: we preserve our bodies, we have children, and we try to stabilize the environment around us so that surviving and breeding have a better chance of success. The knowing processes are not preconfigured - they are the custom things we can do at our discretion.

We don't have wings or claws because we're not meant to have a fixed amount of processes that confine or limit us. We are meant to discover new processes to build value that are limited only by our versatile physiology. Being bipeds, for example, leaves us the freedom to use our very adaptable hands to do a vast variety of activities. We've done so over the last few centuries in order to exponentially expand the number of complex forms being created (e.g. technology and art). Adding new processes to our natural (think, baby) blueprint is what I mean when I say that we evolve ourselves over the course of our life.

In the beginning of humanity, we spent most of our lives in the doing flow like the rest of our living counterparts, trying the best we could to stabilize our environment, live, and breed. As we got better at that, each person had more time freed up to pursue processes of their own design and create additional value through creating new forms. Any time we are engaging in processes that require knowledge we weren't born with, we are creating value through the knowing flow.

If we've been given all this flexibility, which custom processes should we add to ourselves? Whichever ones we are drawn to or are most interested in! Knowing type processes must be built from objective knowledge you draw from the universe, which we search for when we are in the thinking realm. Because you have infinite flexibility in the thinking realm to pursue whatever kind of knowledge you want through simulated experience, the "right" knowledge to search for is whatever you feel most intuitively drawn to. If you are honest with yourself and follow your instincts, you will be searching for knowledge that best fits your unique genetics and associated strengths and predispositions. Because every person is different, you can intuit that each person is perfectly suited to combine knowledge in a unique way. By following exactly what you want, you will guide yourself to collect and combine the right kind of knowledge throughout your life to create a set of processes that not only fills you with passion and joy, but also provides the most value to the universe when you flow your knowing energy through them.

When you first learn to ride a bike, you must think about the mechanics of it, as well as how to combine your body with the machine so that you can achieve effective motion. Once you get the hang of it, you begin to know it, and then you don't have to think about it, you just hop on the bike and begin action. This is a simple example, but it effectively illustrates the pattern of how humans create every new process in their lives: think, know, act.

When you want to do something outside of what nature originally provided you the processes to do, you must first think and collect objective knowledge about the new activity. When you have collected enough knowledge, you switch from thinking to knowing, and then you can route some of your doing flow to the knowing flow to enable a new process that allows you to perform new actions. When you first try to do the new activity, your knowledge may be incomplete, so you will oscillate between thinking and knowing processes until you achieve a level of complete knowledge (mastery) of the new process, at which point you can do that process without thinking about it any longer.

In Gretchen Rubin's book, *Better Than Before: Mastering the Habits of Our Everyday Lives*, she describes how to effectively create new habits by limiting our ability to think before we act.

For example, if you want to start exercising every day, you are more likely to be successful by committing to doing it every day at a set time without negotiation. If you give yourself the option to think about it too much in terms of when you will, or how you will, or what conditions will precede doing exercise, you will be much less likely to form the habit.

I found this insightful because, when I thought about it in terms of process, it helped me to articulate what we've been discussing: *that new processes are successfully enabled by knowing, not by thinking*. In fact, we now know that the process of thinking actively stops the process of knowing or doing. Counterintuitively, to do anything well, you need to think about it as little as possible. Nature's energy of doing complements and feeds your energy of knowing, but neither can flow through you if you step out of nature's flow into the thinking realm.

Joy comes from fulfilling our purpose of creating new form, but if you constantly interrupt your energy flow by thinking, it is difficult to achieve strong flow and consistently transform your energy into value. This constant interruption of our ability to fully fulfill our purpose can lead to anxiety and unhappiness, as we find ourselves trapped in the thinking realm of "should have" and "what if" or simply "don't know".

I'm not suggesting you should never think. Once you understand the patterns of flow, it becomes more intuitive that to increase your energy flow, you must think with intent and do so in uninterrupted blocks of time when possible. It follows then that whenever you return to nature's flow from the thinking realm, you should also try to remain there uninterrupted, wielding your new knowledge for as long as possible before returning to thought. Balancing the knowing and thinking flows this way is applied in the same way for any activity, be it riding a bike, executing a new process at work, or learning something personal like cooking or knitting.

Have you ever been passionate about an activity that you feel mastery of, and achieve a state of flow while doing it? In conventional psychology, the idea of "cognitive flow" is well established. We have likely all experienced it at some point or another—usually when engaging in an activity we deeply enjoy and are highly interested in. Flow is typically experienced as a state of being in which one is fully immersed in the doing of an activity without needing interruption for additional thought, instead operating with total focus on the task at hand.

During my MBA program, I did a semester of independent research where I studied and published a paper on cultivating employee passion. It was at this time when I first learned of this concept of "flow" and the anecdotal evidence that pointed to its definition. It stuck with me at the time, but it wasn't until years later that I better understood the process and energy mechanics that describe this state of being.

When you release the need for thinking and deeply engage in knowing processes, you begin to immerse yourself into the flow of nature to channel doing energy into knowing energy. In this state, time disappears as your attention is fully present within your body, and hours can go by while you continuously transform that energy into value. This is what people describe when they observe "passion"; they have increased energy and they experience the timeless joy of fulfilling their purpose in creating new form.

I have spent a lot of time in the thinking realm before and during the writing of this book. When I finish synthesizing knowledge and return to actualize my knowing energy flow, I have found myself throughout the writing process experiencing those timeless periods of productive writing in a state of flow. To me, it reinforces that I have discovered knowledge that needs to be created, because I feel endlessly energized; as if the computer is desperately trying to pull the words from me. It is an amazing experience, and one that I hope to extend to other activities with increasing frequency.

This feeling is in stark contrast to other activities I've tried to engage in throughout my life, where the constant itch to go back into the thinking realm plagues me throughout the activity. I've come to realize this is a symptom of trying to activate the knowing flow with subjective or incomplete knowledge. If you try to enable a new process in yourself, using anything but objective knowledge, you disrupt your knowing flow which prevents the creation of value. When you expend energy that does not transform into value, you have set up an obstacle to your energy flow, and frustration and energetic tension is the result.

Whenever we enter the thinking realm, we have a chance to simulate experience and discover new units of objective knowledge, but also run the risk of unintentionally mistaking the results of simulated experience for objective knowledge. This is the experience of feeling like you know something and then later realizing you were wrong. For example, if you think that $1 + 1 = 3$, you can start building processes on that foundation, but will quickly find your flow disrupted as all your processes will produce less or no value. This should drive you to go back to the thinking realm to reassess until your new process can improve.

When you start to internalize this dynamic (that obstacles in your knowing flow encourage you to move back to the thinking flow), you should be able to more easily identify passion when it occurs as a continuous and strong knowing energy flow. Alternatively, you will more easily identify when there are obstacles to flow as soon as you feel energy being drained from you, despite being in your knowing flow. From here you can immediately acknowledge that some of what you thought was objective knowledge, might need to be reviewed in the thinking realm before continuing to waste energy in the current process.

When I reference objective knowledge, I'm talking about information that is inherently true from the perspective of the universe, the source of all knowledge. Objective information is that which is not influenced by personal feelings or bias – it is inherently true and accurately describes the reality in which we find ourselves. When the pattern gave us the ability to jump to the thinking realm, it gave us access to all the knowledge of the universe, needing only to be discovered in actionable units. Complete packets of knowledge found in this way act as the foundation to evolve ourselves back in reality. If we do it right, we can efficiently transform those packets of knowledge into new processes, which we can then meaningfully actualize through the use of our knowing energy.

One of the most awe-inspiring dimensions of the thinking realm is that it acts as a cosmic library that can be shared between all humans in the absence of time. When any of us uncover objective knowledge and bring it back with us, we can then create something with it in the real world. Those real-world artifacts, books for example, are then left for children of the next generation to pick up, read, and then go to the thinking realm to confirm the objective nature of the content, without having to discover all over again the discrete knowledge units that were synthesized to write the book in the first place.

Objective knowledge is always relevant and exists perpetually in the present, because it accurately describes some facet of the universe which will never change and doesn't experience time. In this way, we as a species can continually uncover objective knowledge with increasing effectiveness with each subsequent generation. This will provide cumulative efficiency for the evolution of human processes and form.

In writing this book, I am flowing energy through my knowing processes to bring physical form to the knowledge I have discovered in the thinking realm. My hope is that you will absorb some of my thinking through reading, validate the objectivity of it in the thinking realm with much less effort required, and then use it to evolve yourself much faster than I could. You will not have to spend years coming in and out of the thinking realm as I did to uncover the same knowledge. It is in this way that knowledge is "mined" out of the thinking realm and then left there in a more synthesized form for future generations to pick up as needed, helping them continue the pattern.

In present society, we have more room than ever to evolve new processes, because our foundational doing processes take very little energy due to the advancement of civilization. Ideally, this means we could evolve more complex processes faster, and find even more joy than ever before in fulfilling our purpose to create.

Unfortunately, when observing what is considered "normal" behavior today, it is not the case. In some ways we are becoming more sick and depressed than any other time in history. I wish I could say that most people only struggle with occasionally pulling back bad information out of the thinking realm, or that they sometimes stay there a little too long playing with simulations that aren't designed for objective knowledge discovery (such as creating personal judgements and expectations without direction), but the sad reality is that many of us spend the majority of our lives carelessly in the thinking realm.

Like the pearl diver who spends too much time in the water, when we spend too much time out of nature's flow, a lot of bad things start to happen. I'm guilty myself of having done exactly this for most of my life, and it is actually encouraged in many ways by modern societal constructs. I'll explain the consequences through the lens of my personal experience.

## DIVORCE

Shortly after college while I was working as a pilot plant engineer, I felt that I had found financial stability within a career that looked to be shaping up with a lot of opportunity. It was at this time I married my college sweetheart and we started to build our future together. She is beautiful, smart, disciplined, and nurturing - I felt lucky to have found her while still so young, and looked forward to going through life and growing old with her. It was within this context that I spent most of my time in the thinking realm, feeling like I had a lot of great things going for me and attempting to figure out how to ensure these positive outcomes I pictured for myself.

If you had looked at my life from the outside, you would have seen a smart, ambitious young man who was excelling personally, professionally, and academically. While that was mostly true with regard to my external activities, the reality was that I was feeling increasingly ill at ease, mentally sick, and generally disoriented as time went on. At the time, I felt that everything I did was normal and I had no concept of human energy flow, or of this notion of coming in and out of nature's energy, so I didn't realize anything was wrong. Things were getting progressively worse as time went on, however, and my wife was exhibiting the same symptoms of unrest. It took me many years of studying energy and process to fully understand what was happening to me during that period. As I continue this narrative, I'll explain to you what happened through the language of process science.

Like playing video games, running simulations in the thinking realm can become very addictive. In a place where you have infinite power to imagine simulated experience, the most alluring experience of all is to simulate your own life. Even as a child, I spent a lot of time doing this, and it carried through to adulthood.

In my adolescence I would idle away in the thinking realm, rewriting my past experiences through simulation; imagining what I would have said differently, throwing the punch that was never thrown, being the hero and getting the girl. Simulating your past in this way is the start of creating the virtual version of yourself. The version that is smarter, cooler, and stronger. The version that always knows what to do and never fails. You become your favorite actor in the movie of your life, and the thinking realm is always there for you to watch this "better" version of yourself succeed, as much as you want.

The counterintuitive thing about simulating your past is that it is probably the most wasteful way to discover new knowledge. We are taught to reflect on our actions to learn, but we've already experienced those events in the real world in the context of our knowing flow and doing flow. What you get out of that experience the first time in terms of helpful information is probably most of what you will get. If you didn't do something well in the moment, trying to extract more knowledge out of the same situation repeatedly doesn't make much sense, particularly when you can simulate anything you want.

By the time I married, I was less interested in re-experiencing the past, and instead I spent a lot of time simulating my future. The virtual me that lived in the thinking realm was my coach and guide, and I ran everything through him first in order to chart how my life should go. I wanted to be a good husband, son-in-law, and father. I wanted my wife to be able to stay at home and not work if she chose. I wanted to be rich and powerful, but still have time to have fun, relax, and raise my children. In the thinking realm, all those things seemed uncomplicated and achievable. Virtual Sam ran through the whole story instantly – he worked hard, got his master's degree, excelled in his profession, took care of his wife and family, and on top of that, he made it all look easy. I spent a lot of time in the thinking realm admiring him, emulating him, and asking him for advice every chance I could.

All this time, I wasn't really learning from this virtual "future self", because he didn't represent any source of objective knowledge; and meanwhile I was spending more and more time out of nature's flow. This disconnected me more and more from the energy of the universe, and from my purpose to meaningfully create complex form. I never would be away from my "better self" for very long. Even during conversation, I would jump into the thinking realm and let him listen, simulate what he would say or do, let him formulate the next witty or powerful response while my body was only half-listening to whatever the other person was saying in the real world.

There were many times where I was faced with activities I didn't want to do, but when I checked in with him, he said that it was necessary, and that the payout would be great if I stayed my course. Because the movie he was in was made mostly by me borrowing from real movies I had seen in my life, he showed me how to lead by aggression, by dominating and exerting my will over others; this seemed to be the fastest way to use our intelligence to achieve our dreams. When this rubbed people the wrong way, my "real" self and virtual self always conferred and decided that it was because they were jealous or less capable, that our actions were justified in achieving the future he promised we could achieve. He was suspicious of people and their intentions, and we reflected often in our time together on the actions of others as they related to our image and status. The simulation he lived in didn't include any real people, so it was easy for us to imagine the worst in others.

In the thinking realm, it is easier to treat the rest of the world as background noise, distractions that take focus away from the star of the show. Reality is more complicated than that – more complicated than we can ever simulate. Trying to simulate your future with a fraction of the variables that exist in the real world is guaranteed to distort your understanding of reality. In the real world, there are other people, and there is incredible diversity in energy and form that exists around you dynamically. Instead of taking this in, I spent most of my time in the thinking realm with myself at the center of the narrative, seeing the details of my future constructed only as they seemed relevant to me and my own success.

And so it began that I would converse with myself. Not in the clichéd fashion, where I would talk to myself out loud and expect a response from the empty room, but by spending time with virtual me in the thinking realm to use his story, his simulated reality, to validate my own experienced reality. He protected me when other people hurt me, and made me feel like the victim when others sought to use their reality to rob us of our path forward. As I continued to fall increasingly into this unhealthy relationship, he began to speak through me. Things would happen in the real world that required me to act, and he would ultimately be the one responding. I wanted to see the movie I had simulated in the thinking realm play out in my reality, so to whatever extent I could, I channeled the virtual me into reality to actualize the future I thought I was destined to have, ignoring any information or input which indicated otherwise.

I spent most of my marriage doing what he said. I worked hard, I went back to school, I got promoted, I bought a house and shared my success with those around me. Every time I checked something off the list and returned to the thinking realm, he would already be three steps ahead, looking behind his shoulder and urging me to hurry up with that easy smile that told me I could do anything because he had already done it. I look back on my experience of reality during that period and can't even remember if what I was doing was creating value or even made sense, because I wasn't even truly there most of the time.

Whenever I returned from the thinking realm, my life felt hollow, inadequate, and meaningless, so I spent as little time in reality as possible. As my perfect marriage and suburban lifestyle continued to progress, my wife and I both felt like there had to be more, that surely there was something missing. Nothing I built or created gave me joy; I was only driven by the thought of the simulation of my life becoming my real life.

My wife did not have a strong simulation of her own, and to me, this made her seem totally lost and confused. Ironically, she was more present and mentally healthy than I was. When she struggled with anxiety or fear about her life, I would urge her strongly to choose and follow her dreams. To plan her future, to set goals and to pursue them. I wanted her to make her own movie, and follow her own star, because that's what I thought would make her happy. After years of living this way, while I was finishing night classes, we were finally to the point where she could quit work, pursue something more fulfilling, and we could get ready to have kids. It was at this exact moment that she left me, and we got divorced.

I immediately fled to the thinking realm where that virtual version of me had a field day making me into the blameless victim. How could she leave me when everything I did was for her and our family's sake? All my family and friends confirmed how loving, generous, and hardworking I was for her benefit. I returned to reality and made her feel all the weight of her decision, called out her selfishness, and tormented her to ease my own pain. I was the hero and she was now the villain who had ruined everything, and she deserved to be punished. The punishment was delivered in subtle ways, sideways comments and accusations. I couldn't be too overt because the virtual me counseled to treat her nicely in the divorce proceedings, so I could salvage my storyline as a virtuous, well-mannered individual. No matter the justification or circumstances, I see now that it was all wrong.

The truth is that throughout all those years I didn't do anything for her, or our family, or even for me. I was just disconnected from reality, to the point of mental illness. Nothing I did was from a drive to create complex form in the present or to find joy through properly channeling the flow of energy through nature;

when I did so it was coincidental. I spent so much of the universe's energy in the thinking flow, and when I returned with what little knowledge I gained from it, I forced all of my knowing processes forward with incomplete knowledge, even though I could feel the obstacles to flow inherent in the activity.

All my actions were driven towards turning fantasy into reality. I was propagating delusion as the purpose behind all my behavior, which is the basis for insanity. There was no place that brought me peace. I was feeling unrest from being ineffective in value creation when in nature's flow, but in resisting the truly value-adding activities which my form was craving in favor of what I thought I "should" want, I wasn't allowing myself to properly use the thinking realm to positively evolve myself either. I was becoming an abomination whose energy was always disrupted and never focused in a single energy flow.

My ex-wife was always more in tune with nature, consistently trying to take me out hiking, swimming, biking, traveling, or generally to experience the world. Spending more time being in nature's energy was not compatible with spending time in the thinking realm, so I resisted. I basically left my wife alone for our entire marriage, disconnected from reality in order to spend time with a figment of my imagination. Even now I can admit that in the context of the thinking realm, there was only me and other me. She barely had a role in the simulation. I wasn't with her enough in reality to know her, acknowledge her pain, or register her loneliness. In that regard, I was largely at fault for her drifting away from me, and all that followed. Despite that sobering truth, some of my friends and family to this day still shun her behavior and applaud my efforts to create the picture-perfect life, because from the outside I was doing everything that makes a good husband by conventional standards. But in hindsight I can see that this is not the full picture. She wasn't addled enough to subscribe to my insane vision of a future I had no possibility of ever predicting or creating.

I was at fault for being too lost to listen.

My story is not uncommon, and as my awareness has increased over the years, I can see others who are going through similar bouts with insanity, spending too much energy and time the wrong way in the thinking realm. Once you get to where I was at that point in my life, it is very hard to separate yourself from the simulation – your mind blurs the lines of simulation and reality.

Entering the thinking realm allows us to feel the incredible amount of knowledge the universe is comprised of, and how little we can know in comparison. Fear of the unknown can be a powerful thing if we let it overwhelm us. Imagining simulations of our lives that play out the way we want them to be is one way to bring a sense of control and knowing to a reality that is complex beyond our individual comprehension. Looking for patterns from the past and contemplating how our choices can impact our future make us feel that we have taken some control of the unknown and offers us comfort.

This glimmer of peace is a trap, as we can only ever know that which is objective, and that always remains in the present moment. The comfort we gain by the illusion of control pales in comparison to the joy of being immersed in the flow of nature outside of the realm of thinking. Still, we live in a time that encourages simulating our futures with five-year plans and ideas about following a "career path" or "finding direction". People are guided from a young age to try to gain false control over their lives through constructing their desired future in their minds and spending much of their energy trying to shape reality to fit some idea of what they "should" want. The result of this attempt at control is what happened to me, where I sacrificed much of my energy tending to my simulated life, trying to gain control over the uncontrollable nature of reality. When you give in to fear of the unknown, it is easier to let the virtual version of yourself take control, allowing you to reside in the shadows of the thinking realm.

When you give up yourself in this way, you go about your life as a puppet to the simulated version of that self, helping him in his attempt to control your reality and force it to match the arbitrary narrative you created in the thinking realm. What happens to you in reality must always be filtered through the viewpoint that holds your simulation together, and conversely, you feel the things that happen to your simulated self are happening to you in the real world. For example, if you feel somebody wronged you several days ago, you can simulate it in your mind and make your body feel anger in your present reality.

When you are oscillating so quickly between your knowing and thinking flows that your simulation and reality start to merge, this is the point at which you have lost touch with nature and reality and have created a life based more on fiction than on fact. This energy flow imbalance manifests itself into someone who lives in a perpetual illusion, always half in and half out of the thinking realm.

Many spiritual authors refer to people in this state as "dreamers" and this world they live in, somewhere between reality and the thinking realm, as "the dream". Reflecting on our pearl diver analogy, a *dreamer* is one who decides to never fully leave the water. Whether he brings back pearls or not, he spends his idle time hanging off the boat with his legs in the water, always ready to jump back in.

Living in the dream means you can never again lay out on the boat and fully experience the warm sun and fresh ocean air, you are always partially bound to the cold darkness and infinite unknown represented in the water beneath. Living in the dream perpetually interrupts our human flow, separates us from the bountiful energy flowing through nature, and makes us ill. In this state, we can never truly be joyful or stabilize our knowing processes to create new form.

I awoke from the dream only a few years before writing this book.

The divorce separated me from my wife, but also from the dream, and for that I am grateful. The divorce and what came after not only started the awakening process for me, but it became one of my greatest teachers of energy and process. For many like me, it is often only the experience of intense pain that makes leaving the thinking realm and returning to reality possible.

Things settled for me a few months after the separation and I realized that the reality of the divorce had destroyed the simulation I had been building for many years. For the first time in memory, I was totally alone. I had lost my best friend; not my wife, but that other me who had lived with me in the thinking realm for my entire life. The richness of my favorite simulation was replaced with the void of nothingness. That familiar place where I would often go to see virtual me running around with our future kids and dogs was now replaced with empty space. Other me was gone because the future he was written into was suddenly annihilated.

I panicked. Everything was lost – I felt like my entire reality was lost with the destruction of the simulated version. Other me had become a part of me, and he was murdered as collateral damage in the divorce. I immediately set to his revival and reconstruction, and I decided he would be a successful New York City player in his next iteration, so I made plans to move to the city and restart. After moving to the city, though, I was deeply unhappy and struggled to reconstruct other me's life with the same robustness that he previously had. I was impatient to regain my simulated form but was constantly tired and intimidated by the labor of it. It was at this moment when I was struggling the most that I–quite accidentally!–started studying spirituality.

Every quarter, I meet with a colleague and friend of mine. As part of our catch ups, we swap books that we have found to provide value adding knowledge. He offhandedly suggested I pick up *A New Earth* by Eckhart Tolle, a book he remembered enjoying in college but couldn't share much about it beyond that.

I read it, and it saved my life.

Tolle's knowledge put me on the path to connect all the process information I had gathered thus far in a way that could be applied consistently to my personal life.

*A New Earth* is a book about universal spirituality, understanding your purpose, and the path to human enlightenment. He discusses at length in his own words the dangers of the thinking realm, and how we are at a time in history where many people are living in the dream and in pain. At first I found it very difficult to understand, but there were certain truths I trusted intuitively and began to integrate into my understanding in a way that allowed my knowing processes to adjust accordingly.

The thing that pulled me from the darkness was his description of the "ego". The ego is Tolle's term for what I have been calling our virtual, or other, self. In the book, Tolle described how leaving the dream was often made easier through pain, especially the pain of having your ego damaged or destroyed; as the experience provides you with a window to see out of the thinking realm and start to separate it from objective reality. In my situation at that time, it resonated clearly that this very thing was what I was experiencing. I'll never forget the feeling of relief—that brought me to tears—when I understood his message about how to rejoin the real world and the flow of nature.

At a time when I was desperately trying to reconstruct my ego, which had been utterly destroyed during the divorce, Tolle advised that this was the perfect opportunity to simply not do that, to embrace reality as it was and let the flow of nature power your actions without unfounded guidance from your simulated self in the thinking realm. He said plainly that the past and future were fantasies, and what I understood from this was that it was only logical to act on whatever information you either knew objectively to be true, or could process in the present moment.

This clicked with all the work I had done as a process consultant up to this point. I would never advise a client to behave in a certain way based on historical patterns alone, nor would I have them bend their business processes to conform to a future reality that present data could not currently support. I suddenly saw myself as a process and the pattern of the universe started to reveal itself to me.

I saw that there is no need to plan for the future, because it will never come. Your life is shaped by perpetually processing the present moment, releasing you from the burden of time and the fear of the unknown that will never be relevant for you to fulfill your purpose.

Fear is something we inherited from the universe as part of receiving consciousness, but it only exists in the thinking realm. To avoid fear, don't think.

This may sound like a useless platitude, but it is profound. Thinking less and knowing more is the path to achieving flow. When you are flowing energy to your knowing processes, time ceases to exist, and with it the fear of not knowing that which you cannot know. If you simulate a future and try to force it to become reality, you will always be afraid of making mistakes or failing to actualize that future, with irrational behavior as a result. How many times have you not done something you wanted to, or what you felt was right in the moment, because it didn't align with your future plan?

By letting go of your ego, you let go of your past and future, and the fear dissolves along with it. I had awakened from the dream, and it felt like I started my life anew. When I woke, however, I found myself disoriented and living with an extremely high rent in the middle of Manhattan. The path from there has not been easy, and controlling my visits to the thinking realm has been a daily struggle. Despite that, I was committed to it, and not only does it get easier with practice, but the interim results have been astounding.

As I began integrating all these realizations, and spent more time outside the thinking realm, amazing things started to happen. Within these next few years, the logic of it all started to make sense in terms of the energy pattern. As I increased energy flow through myself, I became more productive, more adaptable, and healthier.

I'll never forget the first time I actually listened to another person while fully present with them, without moving back and forth from the thinking realm. I was able to more deeply understand what they were saying and develop a meaningful connection with them through conversation – I was generally more aware of them. It was a natural result of not being distracted with how my ego would react or interpret the information. I started to feel like a super version of myself. I was able to take in more information faster, process activities much more efficiently, and generally acquire more knowledge and skills than ever before.

From an outsider's view, my life became much more chaotic, because I wasn't focused on a linear path. I had friends who were becoming concerned about my goals because every month I chased whatever opportunities I felt like pursuing, with wild abandon. There was no need to worry about whether something contributed to my future goals, because I no longer had any. The activities I did week-to-week or month-to-month seemed random and unconnected, but I was thriving and creating form at a rate I had never experienced. Ultimately, I was becoming one with nature: the pattern of activities was too complex to connect the path, but the mechanisms that governed my life were exceedingly simple.

As I fell into new habits and began exploring my new life, the transition made me appear a bit crazy from the point of view of those still living in the dream. I myself was not completely confident in what was happening at the time, which made it difficult to articulate to others what I was experiencing. I soon found myself in a new relationship that challenged me to put the entire picture together.

I fell in love with a woman who still lived deeply in the dream, along with most of her network of family and friends. As someone newly awakened and experimenting with improving my energy flow, I now had the opportunity to study the pattern from a different perspective. Whereas in my marriage I had played the dreamer to disastrous effect, this time around I was experimenting with how to be more present within nature's flow. Because I was acting a bit oddly in this exploratory transition phase, I had to account for my behavior by clearly articulating–to someone still very much living in the dream–why understanding and controlling my involvement with the thinking realm was the right thing for me to do.

We had a great connection when we were both present, but every time she returned to the thinking realm, she was immediately riddled with doubt and guilt. She felt that our differing religious, cultural and ideological beliefs jeopardized her future, as well as present, standing within her community. This created a constant tension as her ego was repulsed by my involvement in her life, but outside the thinking realm we could both feel the strength of our real-world compatibility.

With my new awareness, I could see that she was someone who was bullied relentlessly by her virtual self, as I had been so often before. There were times that it felt viscerally like I was dating two discrete people, but that awareness alone did not help me separate her from her ego. I realized quickly that the internal clarity I had achieved was very difficult to articulate, and the more I carelessly tried to explain myself, the more out of touch with reality and the more radical I appeared.

How do you tell the dreamer, whose whole identity is tied to a simulation based on a time-bound narrative, that there is no past or future and that nothing simulated in the thinking realm has any meaning beyond extracting knowledge? Trying to articulate that message in a way that didn't make me sound reckless, irresponsible, or overly eccentric was challenging, to put it lightly. Despite being a difficult topic, though, we talked about it a lot and the knowledge I gained from the experience of attempting to explain my newfound insight to someone else rapidly accelerated my understanding of the pattern.

The greatest revelation was that my own downfall was to try and explain myself to win her acceptance, which inherently was an ego-driven activity. My own ego, which I was committed to not allowing to re-form in the thinking realm, was harder to control than I had originally anticipated. When her ego talked through her about things I no longer wished to contemplate (like the past and future), I found myself reviving my own ego to frame things in a similar language so that we could communicate more easily. I began to simulate a reality that could merge with her simulated reality as a means to reach common ground. To talk with the dreamer, you must enter the dream yourself, and I did so unknowingly for many months.

The ego doesn't want to talk with someone living most of their life outside the thinking realm, because being immersed in nature's flow is the antithesis of the ego and it views that person's entire way of being as a threat to its very existence. The complexity of reality vexes the simulated self, whose existence is based on not acknowledging or accepting that everything in life is outside of its control. The ego sustains itself with fear of the unknown, because fear is what keeps you coming back to the thinking realm for comfort and assurance that the unknown is under control.

This perpetual state of creating fear and managing it is not possible within nature's flow, where there is no unknown or fear of any kind. This misuse of the thinking realm severely diminishes your ability to sense interruptions in your knowing flow, as well as makes it difficult to pursue objective knowledge, as all of your energy and focus becomes consumed in tending to the all-encompassing simulation you believe to be reality.

The more we talked about the future and other topics that only exist in the thinking realm, the more time I spent there–to my detriment. I was trying to explain my seemingly eccentric "beliefs" as a means to connect with her, but the truth was, I no longer held any beliefs at all. To even attempt to articulate the way I was living as a belief system is contradictory to the act of being present. Having a belief implies that you would act consistently over time if presented with different situations, because of a set logic framework that you have adopted as representative of you.

If you are committed to reacting appropriately to every moment as it comes, you are no longer acting within a set framework consistently over time. Committing to being present releases you from classification or obligation of all kinds, especially from any burden to act in a certain way over time to maintain the face of your ego. For someone trying to live mostly outside the thinking realm, you don't need belief, you only need knowledge. As she and I experienced increasing relationship tension, I struggled to understand and balance the relationship between someone dreaming and someone trying to leave the dream, with little success. By the time we broke up, I was again a dreamer myself. I was one of the more confused types of dreamers: one whose simulated self identified as more awake, but this identity was only serving to obscure the fact that I had once again lost my real self in the thinking realm.

I didn't realize this until several months later, when my ex-girlfriend and I met again and had a conversation. Since the breakup, I had returned to reality more fully, steadily increasing my energy flow and becoming more aware of the pattern. Upon meeting her again, my ego (which had been dormant) was triggered and the conversation was shockingly out of my control. I could physically feel my real self shoved into the back seat as my ego dominated the entire conversation in a way that made me feel powerless and mortified.

I became acutely aware of the facsimile of myself that I had created while we were in the relationship, and it was a milestone in understanding my relationship with the thinking realm. I called her the next day and apologized. After that event, I knew the face of my current ego and had to undo what had been done. In subsequent conversations between us, I committed to being present, and the dynamics of the conversation were completely different.

Eckhart Tolle had related this very thing in his book, about the power that presence commands in destroying the ego. I thought I had understood it; but having the chance to live it firsthand was an amazing learning experience that gave me greater clarity.

When you are present, you don't recognize or try to control the future. When your ego wants something that is out of your control, it stirs in the thinking realm and demands to confer with you to argue the point - to convince you to attempt resistance to a reality that can never successfully be resisted. Being present when interacting with another person means that you want nothing from the conversation except to enjoy the presence of the other person. When you are enjoying a conversation outside the thinking realm, there is nothing you should be seeking or wanting, because there are no expectations of how the conversation should go. In conversation like this, you can't resist anything the other person says, because doing so invites your own ego to interject within the conversation to justify that resistance to reality. When you don't indulge your ego to interact with the other person's ego, their ego is also immediately diminished.

I had several conversations with my ex after my initial ego takeover. Each time I felt my ego pulsing in the thinking realm, desperately wanting to explain our (mine and my ego's) point of view and why her current course of action didn't make sense. I didn't let my ego have his say. It's hard to avoid the impulse, but trusting in the pattern and letting the universe unfold around you brings a consistent peace in all that you do. To behave this way will always be better for you, even if you can't understand the complexity of why that is in a given situation.

If somebody is not ready to leave the dream, or let go of their virtual self, there is nothing you can do to accelerate the process, except let them feel the power of presence through you when possible. Being present draws the power of nature through you, and that energy pattern radiates into your surroundings. The more somebody gets a chance to experience that, the more they will be drawn to it in their own way, in their own time.

My relationships with both my ex-wife and ex-girlfriend allowed me to see many of the complex dynamics of human flow in action. Humans are the most complicated organism in the known universe, and their interactions with one another follow suit. In pursuing our purpose to create new form, our consciousness acts as an incredible tool, but one that must not be leveraged carelessly. This is evidenced by the sickness that results from being too long away from the flow of nature; a sickness we can see increasing at an alarming rate. Depression, loneliness, anxiety, and overwhelming fear are all symptoms of spending too much unproductive time in the thinking realm.

Many spiritual teachers have missed something fundamental in explaining how to become more present and mentally healthy. The practice of meditation, or any other means of growing your awareness of nature's flow, presumes that you will always return to the thinking realm, that to think is our default state. This is an error which hearkens back to René Descartes' famous pronouncement: "I think, therefore I am." (Tolle has given a similar critique of Descartes' observation, reflecting on the fact that thinking is not what makes us - our existence is not associated with our ability to think). We are trained to consider being present as an exercise, and we congratulate ourselves once back in the thinking realm for our limited efforts to know the flow of nature. Because this is so unfamiliar to us, many people struggle to recognize the feeling of being present, and therefore have difficulty gauging whether their meditative practice is effective.

The reality is that you are always present, except when you go the thinking realm. Presence is not something you have to discover or find, it is the natural state you find yourself in when you don't think – when you clear all the simulations out of the thinking realm. Meditation is very beneficial but should be thought of simply as the practice of not thinking, not the practice of becoming more present. In this way, meditation doesn't need to be a focused activity, but should instead be a constant effort to regulate the wasteful allocation of energy to the thinking flow.

Don't make the thinking realm your home base. When you are not thinking you are in a state of knowing and are drawing on the energy of nature to feel joy in the timeless act of creation. The pattern prescribes this to be our natural state of being. It is the energy flow we are born into, and the same one we will return to completely when our form ends. Nature's doing flow and the human knowing flow should be considered our resting energy flow, rather than the thinking flow.

Every time you think, it is an opportunity to be aware of the separation of yourself from your physical form and a chance to reflect on what you are doing in the thinking realm. Every departure should be with intent to receive knowledge and return to your knowing flow, and you should consider the decision to think to be a serious one every time you do it. Practicing the constant moderation of thought is the true path to presence. If you are coming from where I came from - total addiction to the thinking realm, or living in the dream - what I'm suggesting is a daunting prospect because the place where you want to go to rest is the opposite place that you should. I can say from personal experience that every day that I acknowledge the pattern and choose not to indulge so carelessly in thinking processes, it gets easier, and my energy flow improves. Once you return more regularly to nature's flow, the flow of energy through your body will increase and you can more fully and effectively express yourself through the creation of complex form.

There is no form more complicated than the bond that exists between two humans. Integrating your process with another human process requires a lot of thinking flow and can overwhelm those who aren't prepared for the exercise. I hope that sharing some of my personal experiences of creating human bonds will help you see the pattern and find your own window out of the dream.

## PURPOSE

We know the universe prioritizes sending energy to processes that create value by evolving into increasingly complex form. Nature was the first living process to receive concentrated energy from the universe, and now human processes take some of that flow from nature and can more effectively create complicated forms through our thinking and knowing energy flows.

Our purpose as a living process is to meet the value demanded by the universe. To do anything else would mean that the process that represents you is ineffective, and you will no longer be able to benefit from the energy flow from the universe. This is why it is so important to understand human flow, and it is the reason that carelessly over-thinking is the most certain way to deprive yourself of the universe's energy, and weaken your process. In a simple way, all you need to trust about your purpose is that the more form you create, the more energy you will receive, and the more abundance will manifest itself in your life in every way imaginable.

You would think that with a universal purpose so simple and flexible, we'd all get it right: build form like crazy, and be happy all the time. Why, then, is it so confusing and difficult?

It's because we're the first organism created with the ability to think, to the extent that we can. As a first iteration of this process model, the ability to think is a crude mechanism that must be switched on and off, as we can't know and think simultaneously in the way that nature can perpetually do and change.

Most of our stress and confusion in life comes from not being born with an instruction manual on how to control or use our thinking flow. Our process was designed to allow us to think so that we can evolve new processes throughout our life and maximize our value creating potential. If we correctly balance our thinking, knowing, and doing flows, we can expend energy very efficiently, implementing knowledge into effective form-creating mechanisms. If we balance the flows incorrectly, we end up adding less value than we normally would as an animal, by thinking too much and not taking the value of that thinking and integrating it back into creating.

Think of it like investing money. You have two investment options with money: invest in yourself to support your basic needs and learn new things, or invest in assets that grow more money for you, like real estate or business. How you choose to invest will change depending on where you are in your life and what you are doing. In the beginning of your life, you don't have many processes to make you money, so instead of investing what you make into assets, you spend all of it directly on yourself to keep your basic processes going (spending money on food, rent, etc.) while you evolve new processes that give you extra skills and abilities. Examples of money spent on evolving new processes would be to go to college, directly learn a new skill, buy a new tool, or have somebody with more knowledge train you to do things you don't know how to do.

As you gain more skills and knowledge, you make a higher return when you use those things to do whatever it is you wanted to do with them. This creates extra money which you can now invest in assets, while continuing to use a minimum amount of money to support your basic needs and allow you to continue doing the processes you already have. When you start investing in assets, you can generate enough return to support your basic needs and make additional money; and then these assets also can begin to grow money passively. As you get to the end of your life, you can stop investing in your self-development outside of supporting basic needs, and simply let your assets generate enough money for you to live comfortably until the end of your life.

There is a balance to this investment pattern that makes intuitive sense based on the way our lives are structured. When you are born and have no value to add besides existing as raw potential, you invest everything in yourself to grow. As your life evolves, you spend less money investing in yourself and more money investing in other forms that will return benefits to you that reflect your contribution to their creation. If you follow the balancing logic, you will spend enough money on yourself to achieve your potential, and then spend the rest of the money you make investing in new forms, which can be immensely rewarding depending on how valuable and complex those forms are.

Investing in yourself versus the creation of other forms is exactly parallel to how we spend our energy on thinking (on yourself to evolve) versus doing/knowing (actively creating new form). Not only does this prioritization of your energy flow match the investment pattern exactly, but it also follows a similar pattern of rewards. The time you spend thinking can evolve yourself, but true wealth is only attained through investing in creating new form. When you fulfill your purpose to provide value to the universe, value is returned to you in abundance. To extend the analogy, if you irresponsibly allocate your money throughout your life, only routing it to sustaining and indulging yourself, the result at the end of your life is poverty and unhappiness.

How do we navigate the resource balancing act? With money, it is through financial literacy, or understanding how money flows and is nothing more than tradable energy within our man-made economy. With energy, it is through learning and applying process science. Those who handle their money poorly, typically do so because they don't understand how to balance their investments throughout their lives in a way that promotes the accumulation of wealth. It's not that they don't want to have more resources; they simply lack the understanding to actualize financial success. Those who don't balance their thinking and knowing flows well end up living a life in fear and energetic disruption because they don't have the knowledge to manage their energy flows any other way.

Nature is born a completed puzzle, the entire picture of its life is set at birth, and all its energy is routed to manifesting that picture. A tree doesn't need to think about how tall it will be or how many leaves it will have; it only changes energy into form based on its process and becomes a fully manifested tree as a result.

It is different for humans. We are born with part of our puzzle started, and it's up to us to find and fill in the missing pieces that best complete the picture. To find a new piece, we go to the thinking realm and search for it. Once we find something, we bring it back and put it with the other pieces to see if it fits. If it doesn't, we should discard it and find more pieces. If it does fit, you still go find more pieces to continue to complete the picture. As the picture fills up, you don't have to go back to the thinking realm as much, and you start, like nature, to fully embody your perfect process picture.

I find it helpful to think about the different cycles of our lives in terms of the energy pattern. At birth, you are one with nature, completely in your doing flow to keep your form alive, the most value you can create at that stage. In your teenage years, the balance shifts to mostly thinking as you discover how to evolve into the most efficient process you can be. As an adult, you spend more time in your knowing flow, creating value, but still having room to explore the thinking realm to complete your picture. As you become a mature adult, you spend less and less time thinking, and more time knowing and doing, fully manifesting your purpose to create.

The path to enlightenment is the path to fully realizing your purpose to create. As you discover which processes to add to yourself throughout your life, you can reduce your time in the thinking realm and remain for longer periods in your knowing and doing flow within nature's energy. As children, we slowly leave nature's flow to discover our unique evolutionary path, but we are destined to return, whether voluntarily, or at the end of your form through death.

In the language of process science, the act of becoming enlightened is to complete your puzzle - to spend your life absorbing the knowledge that suits you, and returning to nature's flow to create complex form. You attain enlightenment when you are ready to use your collected knowledge to perpetually create and no longer feel drawn to add new processes to yourself.

As we leave the conversation of human flow, I also want to briefly speak of the definition of love. I've contemplated what love is at various points in my life, and the definition becomes clearer as I define more clearly what love is not. When I was young, I thought hate was the opposite of love, but to hate something means that you care about and put energy into it (which then overlaps with the definition of love). So as I grew older that definition didn't seem to fit. For many years, I considered indifference to be the opposite of love because instead of focusing energy or attention to something, you had no feeling about it at all.

As a process scientist, I now understand that the opposite of love is fear. Fear is the only thing that stops us from loving, and this is because fear is the result of being outside of nature's flow. The act of creation is the act of loving and it is our natural state of being – it is the involuntary outcome of doing and knowing using nature's flow. Love brings us passion, joy, and fulfillment. It is impossible to not love when you are in your doing or knowing energy flow, because you will always be doing what you are meant to be doing: fulfilling your purpose. The creation of anything, especially bonds with other people, can only happen with the energy we describe as love.

It is misguided to say that we need to learn how to love; we need only learn how not to be afraid. From the beginning of humanity, we have been learning to create through love, and the energy which flows through our bonds with each other has enabled us to generate complexity more profound than anything nature could do before us. We developed bonds with our families, then tribes, villages, clans, cities, and nations. And within this framework, we eventually grew into organizations – living processes that draw upon collective human energy to evolve and create more than we could as individuals or as a species.

The modern integration of human processes in order to form a larger organized process is called a *business*. Businesses receive energy flow from humans, yes, but that energy ultimately flows through nature and the universe first, just as we humans draw our energy directly from nature. This is the next large-scale evolution of our collective ability to bond to one another and continue the universe's pattern to prioritize and condense energy flow to wherever the most value is being created. Businesses create forms with extraordinary diversity and complexity, and they are transitioning the energy of the universe into the next major milestone in the pattern.

# BUSINESS FLOW

—

"You are not separate from the whole.
You are one with the sun, the earth, the air.
You don't have a life.
You are life."

Eckhart Tolle

## EVOLUTION

As the most advanced stage of this universal pattern we have uncovered, I find business processes to be wondrous and beautiful. Business evolves because humans, who have found passion through their knowing flow, were driven to push their physiological limits of form creation by forming bonds with other humans to create a new type of process.

Businesses are *living processes* that are sustained by human energy; in other words, like everything else in the pattern, they are sustained by nature and the universe itself. Business processes are birthed with near infinite flexibility and capacity to evolve. They are nurtured and grow their form so long as they continue to provide value, justifying the investment of human energy flowing through them. It was in studying business process that I truly began to articulate my knowledge of the pattern, being constantly awestruck by the simplicity that underlies the seemingly infinite variation represented in business forms.

I was lucky that, in my career, I had the opportunity to explore many different kinds of business processes. In every job I held, including the water treatment job, my role had me traveling the world and getting inside businesses with different markets, structures, cultures, and flow patterns. As I did this work, I was able to understand the commonalities between everything I was seeing, and it helped me greatly in understanding the larger pattern.

Interpersonal human dynamics always struck me as an interesting aspect of business, and was something I had to deal with everywhere I went. Working with many different types of executives, some lovable and some contemptible, I developed an intuition for the level of process stress a business was under based solely on the human energy flow I could sense in the management layer. Businesses with good management typically had strong, continuous energy flow and didn't overthink much when it came to managing staff or business direction, while managers who spent much of their time in the thinking realm often managed business processes that reflected the constant interruption in their own energy flow.

One theme I observed was that the ineffective managers I had met over the years were always in a constant battle against the business itself. They prized and wanted more control, but always had less, and fought against the flow for every scrap of it. To maintain their poor processes by sheer will was a draining battle, as they continually put up obstacles to the natural flow of things which the business' energy in turn was constantly working to destroy. If those managers learned to both think and resist less over time, the business itself would improve its energy flow naturally, and in a sense relieve them of their errors in thinking.

What this taught me early on is that humans don't "run" businesses; we are simply integrated as a small part of businesses. Human processes and energy flow weave together to become business processes. It is in this way that we become something greater than ourselves, and we experience a new type of living organism.

We often make businesses into villainous entities, characterizing them as inanimate constructs piloted by greedy or corrupt individuals who seek to subjugate others for their own personal gain. It is easy to fall into this misconception when you observe how money historically flows to the top of an organization, and hear about mysterious CEO types who are thought to drive the direction and processes of the company, often for their own benefit. To suggest, however, that business processes are inanimate is a severe mischaracterization based on a lack of understanding of the pattern.

To suggest that a business isn't alive is like suggesting that we are not alive because the inanimate particles that form proteins, which form our cells, are not alive. But everything that is created from living things is living itself, and by that same logic, business processes are no different from animal or human processes.

From the moment a business process forms, it is a living entity that falls into the hive pattern of consciousness, with humans as the worker ants, or cells of its body. Businesses are supported by nature's flow of energy moving through humans and businesses and are also subject to living and dying; not because of limitations to their physical longevity on the individual level as we see in humans, but based on the amount of value they produce - a function of how continuous and strong their energy flow is.

Frederic Laloux wrote a visionary book in 2014, *Reinventing Organizations*, in which he discusses the firm as an organism. His book had a tremendous impact on my understanding of the pattern, as he also reached back in history before the evolution of business to address the human-specific pattern of forming organizations. This book resonated with me greatly. Laloux wrote at length about organizations that were achieving unprecedented productivity and process effectiveness through modeling themselves more as an organism and less in a classic "top-down" structure. The logic that governed the new organizational structure, which he calls an "evolutionary teal" organization, correlated to a structure informed by the process improvement methodology that I was developing independently - designed to increase energy flow through businesses to enhance value creation.

One of the critical insights from Laloux's book was an acknowledgement of the living will of the business, to the point where he recommends the exercise of keeping an empty chair in meetings, in order to simulate the business' consciousness sitting and coordinating with the team. I interpret and summarize Laloux's advice as promoting the need for listening and taking direction from the business itself – it will tell you what needs to be done to evolve its own processes, we just need to get out of the way.

For us humans to think that we can control a large business process, it is as if our individual cells were trying to dictate the behavior of our body – it would result in chaos and reduce our energy flow. Listening to and channeling the will of the business may seem like a silly concept to put into practice, but it is the necessary outcome of following process improvement principles guided by energy management.

Understanding and working with business consciousness is simply the intuitive way to do what logic is guiding us to do anyway. The fact is, however, that most business processes are not managed this way today, and as a result many businesses struggle to control and improve their processes.

Why is it that most businesses today don't reflect an evolutionary teal structure? Eventually they will, and the pattern is moving us that way, but the reason we don't see it yet is because we are currently in the middle of this gradual transition. Understanding the variation of business process states today is actually about understanding the transition states which exist within the evolution of the universal pattern.

Business processes have been evolving in tandem with humans since we first started combining our individual processes to make integrated ones. These processes reflect the input of human energy that flows through them, but they are not limited to human physiology, which therefore creates an opportunity for an evolutionary divergence. This means that as energy flow slowly condenses from humans into business, these processes are starting to evolve from being more human-like to becoming something greater than human.

This exactly mirrors the pattern of how nature first condensed energy to form humans. As the energy flow through nature became more condensed, more complicated forms eventually led to the human emergence in the pattern, a form that could no longer be comprehended from nature's perspective. As the energy flow through humans becomes more condensed, business processes are also starting to increase in complexity beyond human understanding. If you think about the first ancient hominids as nature's precursor to the arrival of humans, similarly you should look at modern business as the precursor to the next great milestone in the pattern; the business equivalent of Neanderthals.

To help me articulate the transition states leading the universal energy from humans to the next milestone, I found another great teacher of process in *The Righteous Mind* by Jonathan Haidt. Whereas Laloux studied the pattern starting from the first complex business-like organizations, Haidt went even further back and looked at group behavior in humans from the beginning of our evolutionary history - from a biological and psychological perspective. Haidt's work reminded me of the gradual nature of evolutionary change and made clear to me that in terms of the pattern, human processes have only gradually departed from animal processes - it is not as if humans suddenly became modern humans, which are so radically different from our counterparts in nature.

As we have matured as a species, the balance of uniquely human processes versus our inherited animal processes has slowly shifted to be more human, because the knowing flow can create more complex form than the doing flow, and energy flow is prioritized, or pulled, into it. As humans further condense energy into the knowing flow, integrated business processes are the next transition vehicle that the universe can again rebalance. The first businesses were therefore predominantly balanced to reflect the human knowing flow. But over time, this will shift and the typical business will be more in the business equivalent of the knowing flow, the operating flow. This rebalancing is the mechanism that will bring about the next major emergence event from the pattern.

Because the rebalancing is happening right now, it is important to acknowledge your place and purpose in the pattern so that you don't spend your entire life opposing what is inevitably coming.

Resistance to the flow of the universe will inadvertently weaken or forfeit your opportunity to create value, which will interfere with your ability to experience a joyful life. What Laloux so aptly articulated, in his wise advice to yield control of the business to the business itself was an acknowledgment of what will become a continuing trend: our time as humans in the pattern of leading the creation of form is coming to an end.

There is a limit in how much you can change your processes from where you start in the pattern, which is why acknowledging our animal nature is critical to understanding where we are in the universe's larger pattern. As we create new life that is more complex than we are, humans will always have a base of process which is still animal, and the physical limitations that nature set in us at our creation.

In Haidt's work, he talks about many ancient mechanisms, such as our "hive switch", which is triggered by certain types of group behavior that activate our animal instincts in order to ensure species survival over individual survival. This is only one example of many which illustrates our limits in evolving beyond our animal nature – and these limitations are set in the pattern. The limits are increasingly starting to constrain our ability to compete with or understand business consciousness, as it diverges from human patterns to create value exponentially faster than we can, as a species with a rooted doing flow geared towards the survival of organic form. As business processes take over in the creation of form, it is our purpose to switch to a supporting role so that they can continue their evolution—much like nature did before, when humans began to emerge fully into creation.

Business process is the evolution of the pattern happening now. Early businesses, which were more human in nature, reflected an organizational structure that promoted survival over value creation, and were designed to reflect what we knew about being human. The first business processes had no more information to act on than the humans who ran them, and were often simple extensions of the business owner's individual process as he expanded his ability to create through integrating machines or paying people to carry out mindless tasks. However, as businesses evolve, they are shedding their human qualities and growing into the next stage in consciousness, fueled by our energy flow but also growing of their own accord.

The modern business organizational structure is manifesting as a mature hive mind in which we are the subordinate organisms. Business processes are gaining their own intelligence through technology and tremendous amounts of data that they never had access to before. In this way, businesses are starting to make decisions based on data that make sense for the business, but not for any one individual human working within that business.

From a business ethics and morality perspective, it is important to understand that business processes are evolving into a model more like nature's processes, and therefore don't concern themselves with considering the value of human life, or the wellbeing of any individual who comprises them. As long as businesses receive energy from the human energy flow, they continue to iterate their form in whatever way best supports their own survival and the creation of more complex forms. They are amoral, not good or evil, and will continue to have a greater impact on human life as they become a superior vehicle for the universe to continue the pattern. To judge a business based on human ethical considerations only distracts us from accurately understanding the true contribution a business has to creating complex form as it grows.

The will of the business grows more powerful as a company grows, to the point where even though there are many management layers in place, it is difficult to force the evolving organism to do something that it doesn't want to do. As I work with many different companies, I see the transition to this phase of the pattern proving difficult for some business owners, who fight the need to surrender authority and control to the business itself.

These more human-informed businesses are quickly being out-competed by their more organic counterparts which have better energy flow, and will eventually leave the market unless they can similarly evolve. In the case of Buurtzorg Nederland, a company reviewed in Laloux's book, they formed as an evolutionary teal organization in 2006 with 7 employees. Within 10 years, Buurtzorg had 14,000 employees (of which only 60 are administrative) and is the definitive market leader in its space, out-competing all other more traditionally-structured businesses.

Business processes are a logical next step in the universe's pattern because they take the same mechanics established with nature and humans, and further improve upon both of these in a predictable way. Businesses are like nature, in that they can do and change simultaneously, but they are also an upgrade from nature. Each business can do and change within a single organism – they are not tied to nature's restriction of changing only through generations. Their process is superior to humans as well, because they do not have to switch between their knowing and thinking flows to evolve; they can continue to operate while they change. Also, unlike humans, they are not constrained by the necessary doing processes that support physical survival and breeding – they are not locked into an animal nature.

Business processes are born without physical boundaries. They are only limited in changing their processes by how much they can transform while still maintaining strong enough value creation to sustain their energy flow. Businesses don't have scarcity to their form like humans, so they are without time or fear, and exist only to consistently produce value.

We have already discussed how humans spend energy in the thinking flow, to discover new knowledge, and then bring it back to integrate into doing and knowing processes, which is where the energy is able to create value from that knowledge. Businesses continue this pattern, but instead of the human flow paths of thinking flow and doing/knowing flow, businesses have their own flow paths called the operations flow and project flow.

When the business takes its knowledge and creates value, it is spending energy in the operations flow, much like the human doing/knowing flow. When a business spends energy in projects, this is similar to a human spending time in the thinking flow. Businesses spend energy in the projects flow in order to think and integrate knowledge in the form of new processes back into its operations flow.

Because the "cells" of the business "body" are humans, the business gains the advantages of human flexibility and diversity, but at a much greater scale. The only relative weakness that businesses have is in their human components; because humans can intermittently leave nature's flow, disrupting their own energy flow and the business's as a result. It stands to reason that at the most basic level, in order to improve the flow of energy through a business, we must increase energy flow through its human parts, while also increasing flow at the business consciousness level. Managing energy flow through a business must therefore always be considered on both dimensions - the human level and the business consciousness level.

As the universe reliably evolves based on the pattern of value-based energy prioritization, business is replacing humans as the next process that improves upon current (human) capabilities. Though the next great evolutionary milestone hasn't been reached yet, the pattern would seem to indicate that the next emergence event will be what technologists call "strong general intelligence" (a type of artificial intelligence (AI)). This refers to the "intellectual" part of a machine which is capable of human-level thought. In other words, an artificial intelligence of this kind would be a machine which experiences consciousness like a human can, but which is not limited by human biological constraints.

From my understanding, a successful artificial intelligence (AI) will be able to think and know simultaneously with uninterrupted energy flow. Because strong AI would also have a new, inorganic physical form (in other words, one which is not based on nature's foundation process), it would no longer need to draw its energy from nature or humans. This would make it unlike current business processes, which rely on the energy flowing through humans into the business process. It would have no scarcity to its form, no fear, and its consciousness would be at a level beyond our understanding. Such a form would continue the pattern with an incredible rate of value creation.

In any case, the potential development of business processes into a higher intelligence which does not rely on human energy is still very much a speculation based in the future, and is my own conjecture.

For now, though, we can better understand our place in this ongoing trajectory of evolving ourselves into business processes. To fully manifest our purpose as humans, we must contribute to increasing energy flow in business processes, so that they too can grow and fully manifest their purpose. This is a special time in human history, where the time and energy required to support processes larger and more intelligent than our own has presented itself, and we should be enthusiastic about contributing to the next phase of the universe's evolution.

## OPERATIONS

The *operations,* or *operating, energy flow* is the business process equivalent of the combined knowing and doing flow for a human. It represents the beating heart of the business. If the energy in the operating flow stops, the business dies. The operating flow is what transforms most of the energy the business receives directly into value. Its energy flow pattern is truly a combination of the doing and knowing flow, because the survival and evolution of operating processes is dependent only on the application of business knowledge towards value creation – the functions are not separate like they are in humans.

There are two types of energy needed to power an operating process. One is the money that comes in from humans via the market ("customers" paying for the value created), and the other is labor from the humans enabling and performing the process within the business ("employees" sending their energy through the business to create that value).

*Money* itself is nothing more than a physical form of energy. We give energy physical form as currency so that it can be traded outside the moment of value creation. When you put energy into a process in the form of labor, the money you receive as compensation is meant to reflect the value you contributed to the process overall. Once received, you can take your money energy and flow it into other processes in exchange for value back to yourself. In theory this enables you to maintain and improve your form and continue producing more value as a result. In this way, money energy largely flows from business to business, and it is through business that humans generate money in the first place, by supplying the labor needed to build business forms.

Labor from the business perspective is *the act of engaging human knowing processes to create form as part of the business process.* The amount of value created with your knowing processes should be reflected by how much energy flows back to you. This brings us back to the idea that the more you engage your knowing processes to create valuable forms, the more abundance is created.

If you single out specific operating processes from different businesses, it is easy to question how certain business processes are contributing to value creation – from the human perspective. For example, industries like tobacco, pornography, and alcohol could easily be accused of creating negative value because these products arguably don't make us healthy or improve society in a moral sense.

Because business processes are amoral, however, they will continue to grow as long as human energy *in the form of money* flows through them. The contribution to complex form is ultimately driven from the universe's perspective, which doesn't consider individual human life the same way we do. Even if the benefit humans seek is indulgent, such as the high from nicotine, sexual stimulation, or inebriation, as long as the cost justifies the investment, value is created for the humans supplying energy to the process. In other words, as long as someone is willing to pay for the output of your business process, it will continue to create value.

As a result, the business fulfills its purpose of creating more complex form as it evolves to meet human demand. You may look at the tobacco business and marvel at the complexity of its process as it becomes one of the biggest industries in existence. Despite the benefit of cigarette production being questionable from a human perspective, I know firsthand from living and doing my MBA in Richmond, Virginia (Marlboro's headquarters) that the business has evolved many complex processes, and gives back to society and other businesses in many ways, because of the massive energy flow it receives.

Remember that important law of energy flow: *the universe will always prioritize energy to processes that consistently create the most value when evolving forms.*

Like our study of nature, it is not a matter of questioning whether value is being created within a stable process, but how the value is being created, and in what form. We may be killing ourselves through indulgence as a species, but the consistency of our energy contribution to these processes has a higher order of value creation for us to discover.

I'm discussing "unsavory" industries to illustrate a crucial point about the study of how energy flows through the universe. In order to truly understand this science and gain key insights about how business consciousness works and creates value, your approach must be from a mindset of suspended judgement and fundamental understanding of the pattern.

Don't question the value created from consistent energy flow; rather, seek to understand it.

Human energy flows into businesses that create value from the human perspective, but our perspective of value is ultimately subordinate to the universe's pattern of value creation. The value we seek from a business either helps us become healthier (mentally or physically), which reduces cost in our doing flow, or more productive or knowledgeable in some way, which reduces the cost in our knowing flow.

Executing our doing and knowing processes as humans happens in service to the universe, so it follows that a business's operating flow is also aligned in meeting that same goal, despite the incredible diversity in what humans perceive as valuable. If a business was born completely from irrational, non-value adding human demand, it is typically not going to survive long in the marketplace, because from the universe's perspective it represents an obstacle to flow. The universe's flow will always destroy any obstacles that present themselves. Understanding that business operating flow serves the pattern, not humans, is an important foundation to contemplating the structure of the different layers within operating processes.

Operating processes are best described in three layers. These layers always exist simultaneously and describe all processes, including natural and human processes, but are more appropriate to analyze in the business context. In the operating energy flow, the layers can begin to separate due to the amount of flow obstacles in the process. There is an upper threshold for the degree to which these layers can diverge before the business dies. Because of this, for humans to work with or manage operating processes, they must understand and manage the layers separately.

The three layers of any process are the workflow layer, the design layer, and the value chain layer. The workflow layer describes the physical behavior that changes the environment in which the process occurs – this is how value is given form. The *workflow layer* is defined as *the observable and tangible activities performed by people and machines working together to enable the process to exist in the physical world.*

The design layer is a *theoretical representation that describes the workflow intent, activities, and their relation to each other in time and space*, and is typically given form through a picture, or process map/diagram. Having a design layer allows people to see and work with business processes without having to go and observe the process everywhere it's happening in the physical environment, which is becoming increasingly difficult as businesses are spreading out geographically through digital mechanisms.

The *value chain layer identifies, filters, connects and describes only those activities which directly contribute to the creation of value*. Typically, a design of a process will have many steps, but only a small subset represents the value chain, or those steps in the process that directly produce value.

In nature, where there is no obstacle to energy flow, the three layers are always the same. For an animal, whatever happens physically (i.e., in their workflow) matches exactly with their process design (over which they have no control), which also matches exactly with their value chain (what they were meant to do to produce value). Therefore, the three layers discussion is not relevant to nature, because without its energy flow being disrupted, there is no reason to contemplate the differences between layers.

For humans, there is similar exact overlapping between workflow and design, because whatever we are doing physically at any given moment matches the process design we intended. This is because our physical doing and design intent are controlled centrally by our consciousness. The difference is that humans can disrupt or add obstacles to their flow through thinking carelessly, which starts to cause divergence between their design and value chain layers. If we think ineffectively, and then come back from our thinking flow to integrate process elements that don't add value, we have now created a gap between our value chain and process design layers, which results in wasteful behavior (i.e., process steps which cost energy but do not provide value).

For businesses, however, the differences between the layers can be drastic. This is because humans imagine the design layer on behalf of the business, but this may differ from the actual value chain layer based on the inability of humans to fully understand the consciousness of the business. Humans also have trouble aligning the business workflow exactly with the design itself because it often takes the coordination of many people and machines to bring the process to life in the real world.

You can view the growing misalignment between layers as being directly proportional to energy flow interruptions and the reduction of value creation within an operating process. The reason this happens so often and so noticeably within the operating flow is because humans are the ones who must execute the process. To return to our ongoing hive mind analogy, if all humans are not perfectly aligned with the business's brain or consciousness, chaos and disruption are inevitable results. A dysfunctional business with separation between its process layers is like a brain that can only communicate partially with its limbs, while the limbs themselves also have a level of individual autonomy to do as they please.

Without process continuity and process layer alignment, energy flow is weakened throughout the operating flow. If this happens to the point where no value, or even negative value, is created, energy will stop flowing through the business, and business death will soon follow. Therefore, the operating flow for a business process is always critically important. If the energy flow is disrupted too much, nothing else matters. This would be the equivalent of animals or humans not giving enough energy to their doing process, which is the process meant to keep them alive.

In the case that the three layers have high alignment and the operating flow is creating strong value, the other flow path must then be considered and balanced to ensure business longevity: the *project flow*.

## PROJECTS

The energy that flows through projects is the business equivalent to the energy that flows through the changing and thinking flows in humans. Like all other ecosystems we have discussed, businesses operate in a dynamic environment that is constantly creating new contexts for success. To remain viable in a constantly evolving market environment, the business cannot simply maintain its operating (or "knowing/doing") process as-is; it must also "think" in order to evolve its process by adding new process elements.

Consistent with the universal pattern we have been discussing throughout this book, the project energy flow costs energy, but does not contribute as strongly to value creation as the operations flow, so the cost:value ratio must be balanced. Unlike the operations flow, which is powered largely by energy directly from the market outside of the business, project flow is powered predominantly by internal energy from humans who comprise the business.

Humans who participate in project work for a business are entering the thinking realm on behalf of the business. Their goal is to collect the objective knowledge needed to appropriately evolve the business's process, with the intent to return and integrate that knowledge into the operations flow in order to strengthen value creation.

For example, if a business wants to add a new product to their operations, they must organize a project to think about how it will be done. Once the project is finished, the new process necessary to launch the product must be "operationalized", or somehow brought back into the core operating process of the business, to be effective. This is parallel to how humans balance their knowing and thinking flows, going to the thinking realm to gain knowledge, and bringing it back to integrate new processes into their knowing flow. However, there is a difference between humans and businesses in how the knowledge is integrated back into action.

As humans, we oscillate quickly between thinking and knowing, which causes small interruptions in our knowing flow throughout the day. Because this is normal for humans, these pauses are not perceived as pauses in our actions and thus we largely see our workflow layer as continuous, uninterrupted activity; but in fact it is not.

In business process, however, this interplay between operations and projects happens simultaneously because the operations flow can never stop. This represents a large difference in process management within a business compared to how we manage human processes. Humans can pause their knowing flow while they think, because our doing flow, which we inherited from nature, is automated and largely runs in the background regardless of the activities we're engaged in (for instance, continuing to breathe in and out or one's heart continuing to beat regularly).

Generally, however, a business cannot pause to think. Its operations have to run perpetually, because there is no separation between a business's basic survival activities and the more complex creation of value. This comparison is important, because it is this difference which creates a much more complicated dynamic for how a business evolves new process, compared to both nature and humans.

In nature, animals only ever put uninterrupted energy into their doing processes, because the changing part is handled over generations, and separately from the individual organism. Humans get to stop their processes when their knowing flow seems to be less effective, find new knowledge, and then restart the new process with the freshly informed process elements integrated. Being able to stop the process, and reconfigure it before starting again, makes the evolution process less complicated; but is ultimately less effective because of all the pausing. It would be like having to shut a machine down completely every time you changed the settings. It's less risky in some ways, but less productive in others.

Businesses, on the other hand, must continuously run their operating flow, but also somehow take newly gained knowledge and integrate it into a live process that can never stop. This would be like a human trying to read a book about running, while also in the process of engaging in running activity. We would have to synthesize the book's knowledge in the thinking realm on the fly in order to change our running style in the middle of that same run. This might sound tough, because it is, but it's what every business must eventually do in order to gain stability in its operating flow.

This behavior – the doing (operating) and changing (project) energy flows taking place simultaneously within a single organism – is the new development that we haven't seen before in the universe's pattern. This allows business to undergo dynamic evolution; which, when combined with their absence of physical limitations, makes them the most powerful form in the pattern.

Let's take a physical example of dynamic evolution. Imagine an amorphous physical form which represents a business process, and simulate that it is going hunting for food. This entity can dynamically evolve without physical limitations. Because it sees that its prey is far away and has a head start, it sprouts extra legs to make itself move faster. As it's running, it realizes that its targeted prey is actually amphibious, as the creature it is pursuing slides into the water to get away. In response, the business process entity leaps into the air, sprouts fins, sheds its legs, re-configures its lungs mid-leap, and lands gracefully in the water to finish the hunt.

Even though this sounds like something out of a science fiction (or possibly horror) movie, it conveys at a visceral level how much more powerful this process structure is compared to the one we have currently. Humans can stop what they're doing and evolve new processes at will, but only if we can enable them with our hands, feet, and fixed physiology when we return from the thinking realm. If a human was participating in this hunt, he would have to pause, figure out how to construct a breathing apparatus, gather materials somehow, then build the tool and put it on before pursuing his prey into the water. The business process creature we have described can do all of this in an instant without requiring any additional resource-gathering or pauses to think and build a solution.

With this ability to evolve dynamically comes another new phenomenon in the pattern: *single organism process transition states*. Because operating flow can't pause to integrate project knowledge, the integration of new process information must be done while the operation has stable energy flowing through it. This means that there are transition states which form between the as-is and the to-be processes, since the operating flow must change dynamically in order to transform from one state to another.

In human flow, there are no transition states. Instead, the change occurs as follows: run energy through as-is process, pause, add new process elements, un-pause, run energy through to-be process. This is the "powering down, reconfiguring, power on again" approach to personal evolution which we covered previously. But in a business context, there is no powering down - the evolution occurs while the organism is still continuing to operate as usual (just as, in our previous visualization, the business process entity sprouted fins and grew gills mid-air while still living and breathing and moving as normal).

The gap between the original version of the process (the "as-is") and where it ends up (the "to-be") – when the entity's lungs, for example, were in the process of turning into gills but were not yet fully existing in a gill state – is what we are calling a process transition state. It is the state of being which is experienced by the organism when it can no longer be considered the original version of itself and yet before it has fully developed into the new and improved version.

The existence of transition states in the business organism has a major implication for business process evolution. For a business process to get from an as-is to a to-be state, it acts more like a live chemical system and requires "activation" energy to move from one to the other. This activation requires a surge of energy to power the transformation, because transition states temporarily put the business process in a state of requiring higher energy to be effective.

This is a similar principle to that of inertia as found in nature - in order to change from one way of being into another, such as to move a stone which is currently not moving, an extra burst of energy is required above and beyond the energy being expended to remain in the current state of being. This extra energy is needed to overcome the natural resistance to change which living beings experience. Chemistry works similarly, in that many molecules could get to a more efficient atomic configuration but must receive energy to overcome the activation cost of moving through the transition state to do so.

In the case of a business transition state, this energy surge must come from the operating energy flow, where the business's energy is generated, in order to enable it to transform itself using the new project process elements. To bring this concept back to our crazy hunting business beast, in the moment between dropping its legs and gaining new fins, in this "transition state", it is temporarily more vulnerable in a jumbled state of having a bunch of half-formed and half-discarded limbs. If its transformation was to stop at that very moment, it would be rendered incapacitated.

It is at this moment of transformation and transition, therefore, where energy cannot travel as well through the process (because everything is jumbled and half-formed), that a surge of energy is required to complete the transformation. At this juncture, the organism has no option but to finish integrating the new process elements if it wants to keep on living. Because of this, integrating new process elements has a high degree of risk. If the operating flow cannot provide the additional surge of energy required to integrate project outcomes, this poses a serious threat to business survival.

All these new mechanics unique to business processes provide the structure in which project flows versus operating flows must be balanced. The primary consideration is that the operating energy flow can never stop or the business dies. Anyone deciding to shift human money or labor from the operating flow to the project flow needs to consider the risk of weakening the operating flow for the sake of bolstering the project flow. Like knowing versus thinking in humans, where there is a risk to over-thinking, the most extreme outcome for a business is death if too much energy is siphoned from operations to projects. An example of this would be a huge research and development project that, if unsuccessful, would put the company out of business.

The other balancing factor to calculate is the surge of operating activation energy required to integrate project outcomes and move the process through the transition state. If you don't have enough energy left in the operation for that energy surge after the project itself is over, even if you can afford to shift energy flow from operations to projects overall, the live organism will not be able to integrate the project outcomes and the project will have been a waste at best, or at worst, could kill the business.

It therefore follows that, even though the business process has no physical limits and can take infinite form, it is nonetheless not free to activate its project flow and create new processes recklessly. The right balance of project flow in a business process will maintain an appropriate strength in the operating flow, while also adding valuable process elements at regular intervals to make sure that the operating flow remains viable within its dynamic market environment. For businesses that have very strong operating flow, they can risk taking on more projects because this doesn't risk process survival. Conversely, for young business processes, it is usually wiser to focus on strengthening the operating flow and reduce project flow to a minimum.

It should be clear at this point how distinct the operating and project energy flows are, how they follow the pattern, and how they serve complementary but separate functions. Business processes are extremely complex compared to a single animal or human. A single business organism is more like a miniature version of the entirety of nature than any other form. And yet, despite the complexity and scale of process elements that make up a large business process, there is ever only the two types of energy flows that we have defined here, and the perpetual balancing act between them.

As I grew into process science, this all became clear to me while working with different businesses in different stages of their life cycles. What at first seemed like complete chaos, now reveals itself as these two flow patterns manifesting in different states of organization or disarray. The business itself is always trying to break down obstacles to its own flow and regain structure to support the universal pattern and the individual business' survival.

Sometimes, depending on the humans involved, the business needs significant help in managing its energy flow. This is where process improvement comes in.

Process improvement is the application of process science in the service of identifying and removing obstacles to energy flow in business processes. Removing these obstacles automatically increases energy flow through the business. Increasing flow in turn directly increases value creation. This is what all businesses are fundamentally seeking when they require process help, whether they can articulate it that way or not. Because of the way business processes are structured, they require improvement of energy flow on the two dimensions I referenced previously: reducing obstacles to flow within the human element or "worker ants" of the colony; and, reducing obstacles to its own energy flow at the business consciousness level, which simply means better balancing of its operations and project flows.

## IMPROVEMENT

Practically speaking, improving energy flow in business increases value creation. This value creation not only helps a business survive and evolve, but also translates directly into increased profitability, through both revenue increases and cost reduction across the entire process. At the level we're talking about, it's as simple as that. Remember when I described unblocking my own energy flow and feeling like a superhuman? It's like that with every process, and it's especially noticeable at the scale of a large business process. The business becomes more productive, more adaptable, and is more effective at both learning and pursuing its objectives.

As business value creation goes up, energy (in the form of money) increases its flow back into the business, and the cycle continues until that flow once again becomes blocked or disrupted. It sounds simple enough, but the problem is that process science is new, and there aren't many process scientists out there. This leaves a lot of businesses in desperate need of help, and the need is growing as business consciousness increasingly diverges in form and nature from human consciousness.

To be able to consistently identify and remove obstacles to flow, you must first be able to "see" the flow. For me this has become easier now that I understand the different types of flow and how they work together to evolve the business. I can now walk into a business and use my process vision to see the flow of energy and where it's being blocked.

To understand what it's like to see a business with process vision, let's visualize it. The business process in total is a complex integration of individual operating and project processes, much like the human body is a complex integration of smaller biological processes. Imagine each constituent process as a garden hose that energy flows through. A typical business, when managed ineffectively, is a massive jumble of hoses. Once you can understand the different hoses and see the flow running through them, the work (in principle at least!) is as easy as unbending and untangling the jumbled collection of these energy hoses.

For most people, doing this task without the process science principles and its associated process vision is very difficult, because the business landscape appears chaotic and represents infinite variation and complexity. To achieve my own process vision, I had to synthesize all the knowledge we've discussed up to this point and apply it in practice for many years. The good news is that I've transcribed it all here in a physical form, so that you can also begin to understand process science and start improving processes more effectively on your own. If you've read this far, you already know how to improve human flow (through the cessation of thought); the next step is to apply the process science language to the aspects of business process flow.

Before we get into the process science, I must briefly acknowledge the history and development of process improvement methods. Two of the most well-known of these methodologies are Lean and Six Sigma. When I first drafted the manuscript which would eventually evolve into this book, I included a long section about Lean and Six Sigma, comparing them to the new process science-enabled process improvement techniques we are discussing here.

Even though both of these methodologies are robust and represent the most prominent approaches to process improvement today, they can't compare to the approach to process improvement which applies the discipline of process science. Lean and Six Sigma are tools in a process scientist's toolbox that largely focus on measuring and manipulating only the workflow layer of a business process, with the intent to reduce that business's costs. Process science, on the other hand, offers a completely new approach to analyzing and optimizing the energy flow of an entire business organism through all of its process layers.

I still respect both of these more traditional methods, and I recommend that everyone become familiar with them, at least at a fundamental level. In addition to teaching the language that most process professionals speak, they bring a less abstract level of logic and mathematical rigor to process analysis, which will help you understand the pattern. You will just need to be aware that learning and applying these methods will not help you to holistically understand the business organism; they don't translate particularly well to the increasingly digital nature of business; and their application as a standalone method has proven to have inconsistent results. Once you understand how to manage the different aspects of business energy flow, you will also understand intuitively when to use Lean and Six Sigma principles tactically in order to most effectively remove obstacles to flow. But your first target in process improvement should always be to address the human and business consciousness dimensions at a high level.

When you address obstacles to flow in the human aspects of a business, you are managing the element of "process transparency" within the business process – that is, the hose "unbending" part of the analogy. Imagine a garden hose that is bent, or kinked, in multiple places. Every time the flow of water must navigate a kink it loses energy, in the form of overcoming the resistance to flow caused by following that kink in the hose. Every human within a business who overbalances the thinking flow over the knowing flow represents a kink in the process and creates an obstacle to flow.

Let's take an example: visualize yourself as an individual in a business process comprised of 100 humans. All you know about your job is that your work is to enter data from a piece of paper into a computer whenever the paper is given to you throughout the day. When your eight hours are up, you go home and come back the next day to repeat your part of the process.

In this (extreme) example, you as the employee have no idea what the business is trying to achieve, or how your data entry task is contributing to business value creation. You make up a small part of the business' total process, but the way you perform your task is not impacted by what happens before the paper reaches you or after you enter the data, because you can't see past your desk – you have no process transparency.

In this scenario, you may think you're doing a good job. But in most cases, employees with a poor grasp of the overall process in which they participate actually represent a kink in the business. This is because, without the context to understand why you are performing a given task, it becomes difficult to adjust your approach dynamically if process needs shift or if waste enters into the process. You continue doing the wrong thing or creating unnecessary waste for much longer than you otherwise would need to, because you are unaware that the process is broken. And this in turn disrupts the rest of the process in a ripple effect beyond the immediate task you are assigned.

In order to address this kink, a process scientist would likely recommend improving *process transparency*. *Process transparency* refers *to the degree to which information that describes an entire business process and its value creation objective is complete and available for everyone who is involved in the process.* The lower the transparency, the more likely it is that human energy flow through the business will be disrupted. With higher transparency, the business can more easily enjoy continuous energy flow through its human dimension.

In the example above, it would be easy to think (from the employee's perspective) that you are appropriately busy and productive; however, this perspective is missing important context to actually validate this assumption. Instead, this employee is likely to have a disrupted flow, due to his lack of knowledge beyond the immediate task at hand, or of the value objective he is supposed to be working towards.

Remember, human flow is only disrupted by a person spending too much time in the thinking realm. An inadequate understanding of the assigned task, combined with a real or perceived lack of autonomy to change how the task is done, typically leads to this type of disruption. The worker may believe he is being productive, because he is completing the assigned activity. However, when a person is lacking sufficient knowledge to understand the value he is creating, this typically results in two potential issues: 1) wasted time and energy spent oscillating between knowing and thinking, in an effort to force a non-value adding process without correcting it; or 2) disengagement from the task and procrastination. These are both symptoms of an overbalancing of energy in the thinking realm, and will commonly be the result of low process transparency within a workforce. Let's look at each of these issues separately.

When a worker is attempting a task which he does not have sufficient knowledge to understand or complete properly, he will often end up doing the task incorrectly, or simply be unable to contribute any additional value once his tiny portion of the process is done, since he does not know what the full picture looks like and what the process is trying to achieve. Instead he will end up wasting time correcting mistakes, thinking too much about how to do the task, and/or doing a wasteful or ineffective task for as long as he is charged to do so.

When a worker is spaced out and/or procrastinating, the worker is not engaged with his task and instead is prioritizing the simulations he enjoys in the thinking realm over being present with what he is doing in the real world. Again, this lack of engagement is often the result of an incomplete understanding of the purpose of the task, or not having enough work to do as he waits for the next batch of papers to come his way.

Both of these flow obstacles find their root cause in broken or incomplete communication between the business' consciousness and all the humans that make up the organism. The effectiveness of the business brain to coordinate with the colony is directly related to the level of process transparency; in other words, the extent to which everyone knows what is happening, and why everything is happening, at all times.

Why does a better understanding of the business' consciousness prevent people from negatively losing themselves as much in the thinking realm? When you have this information, your job is never truly "done" because you are now able (and even expected) to always think of new ways within your personal process capabilities to support the business overall, instead of mindlessly processing a stack of tasks until they are complete. Less idle time means less thinking time and more opportunity to create value. You also immediately have more feedback to your actions in order to better align your own process with the overall organism, rather than mindlessly completing a task inaccurately or in an inefficient way.

Understanding why and how the people before you do their work, and why and where your work product goes after it is done, naturally increases alignment and synergy among processes between all workers in the business, as well as enhances the individual's sense of engagement with his work. This means that, as your colleagues change their process, you are now reacting to that change and constantly evolving to support yourself and them; instead of doing the same static process you were assigned over and over without understanding, and waiting for someone to tell you that it's wrong and needs to be changed.

This constant evolution of the business process as the sum of all its pieces greatly influences the overall flow of energy throughout the process. The awareness of your place in the greater business process significantly decreases the likelihood of people living in the dream and having a poor knowing flow because they become aware of how their process impacts the success of other processes in the real world. Process transparency also allows the individual to take continuous action, because you don't need to wait for new information to be given to you to evolve your process for the business' sake. In very process transparent organizations, you always have access to all the available data and knowledge (good and bad) that could impact the business at a given time. Equipped with this knowledge, you are expected to balance your knowing and thinking flow and to synthesize that knowledge into your individual part of the business process accordingly. In a business with high transparency and strong individual accountability, even the least skilled worker on the team (who might do repetitive tasks for the majority of the day) is expected to own and improve his process to be as efficient as possible within the context of the ever-changing business organism.

Increasing process transparency can be thought of as an overarching process design principle. If you let all of your design decisions contribute to net increases in process transparency, you will see improvement in the energy flow of the business no matter what changes you make. Increasing process transparency through process design typically leads to increased authority, autonomy, and data flow to all staff, as well as reduced management, approval, and audit mechanisms. Improving transparency will make improving and sustaining process continuity much easier because in doing so you are removing obstacles to the human level of flow. Regardless of how strong or weak the flow is at the business consciousness level, if the business can communicate easily with all the cells in its body, it will always be more effective in sustaining strong flow.

To address obstacles to flow at the business consciousness level, you will need to be managing "process continuity" within the business process – this is the hose "untangling" part of the analogy. This is similar to the activity of increasing flow within an individual human. Humans, however, can't merge their thinking and knowing flow like businesses can, when they merge and tangle their operations and project flows. If humans oscillate between thinking and knowing quickly enough and for long enough, they find themselves in the dream state, with one foot always in the thinking realm. For businesses that never stop their operating flow, a poorly balanced project flow will simply end up merging with operations. Like two hoses that are tangled together, flow becomes severely impeded and they enter a business version of the dream state where there is a lot of activity, but most of it is wasteful or irrational. This is where *process continuity* comes in.

*Process continuity* measures *the degree to which energy flows continuously through the business process to create value.* Increasing process continuity is largely achieved by understanding, separating, and balancing the operating and project flows in a way that maximizes total flow. Only after that balancing occurs should targeted individual process improvement be considered, although this type of work is commonly what people first think of when considering process improvement (and it does contribute to flow, but only marginally so compared to the consciousness level flow balancing).

As a process scientist starting a new analysis, my first step is to assess the degree of process continuity in the business. I begin by looking to understand where the business organism currently is in its life cycle, balance its operating and project flows accordingly, and only then will I look for obstacles to flow within individual processes. Even then, I only move forward if the business has very specific flow-increasing objectives, as well as a healthy enough operating flow to safely power process evolution.

In the context of improving flow at the consciousness level, I'll introduce a few key concepts specific to the study of process science. The first task that needs to be done at this level is to clearly articulate what the operating flow of the business is. This largely entails defining and validating the value proposition of the business (i.e., "which types of form are you trying to create and why?"), followed by identifying and defining which processes directly contribute to transforming energy into value.

Because I can't speak to the business consciousness directly, I usually start this conversation with executive staff, and have them walk me through their accounting and finances. Tracing the flow of money through an organization typically serves as an accurate representation of where the energy is flowing through the total business process and can provide early indicators of major obstacles to flow.

For organizations that have a lot of unstructured project flow merged with their operating flow, we then discuss how to physically separate the two flows, and place the operating flow under operations management, and the project flow under project management. Both disciplines are well defined, and continuity is increased dramatically as long as both functions are given the right balance of energy to properly meet their value creating obligations to the business. Once the operating flow is separated out, I typically delve more into the energy dynamics within the operating flow itself to further untangle it.

Universally, the more complex tangling within operations is due to "shared service" process elements growing randomly within the "core" operation, or primary operating flow(s) of the company. Shared services are your common corporate functions, such as HR, Marketing, IT, Legal, and Finance. These operating functions typically support the humans that are assigned directly to the core operation in order to enhance their capabilities, so they only indirectly contribute to value creating processes themselves. The reason shared services normally separate themselves into new processes is that there are some economies of scale in coordinating these activities centrally, as opposed to letting the core operating flow scale those functions as it evolves.

This trend is actually reversing as organizations become more organic, like the evolutionary teal organization as described by Laloux. This is because large, unwieldy shared service functions can represent tremendous waste to an organization if managed improperly. In a well-run organism, the shared services functions can remain minimal, even in large businesses. However, this is still a controlled approach - letting them grow randomly within the core operating flow often produces obstacles to flow because both activities have different energy requirements and produce value differently. Once these shared service processes are identified, they should be similarly untangled from the core operating flow (like the project flow processes) and put under distinct management, usually in the form of a corporate structure.

I worked with a business recently where the tangling of all these flows had become a serious problem. As a small company they had strong transparency, but their process continuity was so low that the business was in jeopardy. They are a decade old theatre arts company, and they grew well without structure for many years but more recently had started experiencing reduced profitability to the point that it halted their growth. Their main complaint was that they felt like their staff didn't have clear roles and couldn't understand who they reported to or what their value creating objectives were.

When I analyzed the flows, I could see that the business had gotten to a scale which necessitated more careful human resource, legal, and finance management, as well as more thinking flow to address the shifting market demand. In their case, they had one set of undifferentiated "family style" resources trying to manage everything: the shared services HR, Legal, and Finance functions, the project flow, and the core operating flow. The business demanded it, so they complied, but all their energy flows started merging together because they didn't allow for differentiation or focus within the workforce. This meant that some resources were starting to work on projects, manage their operation, as well as tend to various shared services functions as they became critically important, all at the same time.

When a single human resource must manage all these flows, their productivity goes down and they become overwhelmed. For many of these employees, they couldn't see the fundamental differences in these activities, and they constantly switched gears between them, just to keep the business's head above water. Flow was severely diminished, and the business started to become sick. Within a few months' time of working with them, we were able to untangle all these flows, set up a project and shared services structure, and reorganize the resources to better match different energy streams. From this work alone, process continuity was dramatically improved.

In this case we didn't hire more people, add new technology, or change any of the processes. We simply had to realign the workforce to better receive energy in a continuous way. Often, businesses try to solve flow problems with more resources or technology, only to continue compounding the problem and further extending themselves into debt or energetic disarray.

The untangling activities we just described could take a few weeks or many months, depending on how tangled the flows are and the size of the business. Once they are complete, you have increased flow, and an isolated core operating flow to focus your attention on to further increase continuity. It is through improving an isolated core operating flow specifically that you stand to most directly increase value creation and position the business to further its evolution. At this stage, there are a few critical concepts in energy flow management that will help you navigate the improvement work, mostly applicable to organizing and equipping the human labor in a way that perfectly supports the now clearly defined operating process.

*Operating model* is a term I use to refer to *the plan that describes how people and technology will be combined to collectively and comprehensively enable a business' operating flow.* If you have the operating flow isolated at the design layer, it should describe a continuous series of activities that indicate how energy will be transformed into value. Your operating model should indicate how staff and technology will be associated with all the activities, ensuring that all are staffed adequately and can be continuously executed, based on the strength of flow through the process - this is a major factor in ensuring continuous flow.

At this stage, you don't have to worry about which people go in which role, but rather, focus only on what needs to be done by people versus technology (or a combination of the two) given your current state of resources. The operating model should comprehensively speak to core operations and shared services, but will mostly be designed from the core operating process, which is what defines the life line of the business.

After the operating model is established, the next piece is the "organizational structure", or org structure, which would further organize the human resources to promote flow in their assignment to the human designated process elements established in the operating model. Designing an organizational structure, based on discrete functions called for by the operating model, and the measurable experience and skills needed to perform them, ensures that the org structure is scalable and not based on the specialized or unique skills of individuals.

Many businesses I've worked with assign arbitrary roles to people which are not based on process functions, and this becomes an obstacle to flow. Having fifteen "vice presidents" or twenty-five "junior managers" doesn't mean anything if you don't tie the structure back to process driven requirements. If you can't read someone's title and clearly identify which part of the operating model they are enabling, the organizational structure is a risk to continuous flow, and will inevitably become untenable over time. This is one of the major contributors to the workflow and design layers of business process separating, because as the process changes and calls for new functions, people without clear guidance will start randomly filling the gaps and merging energy flows.

In conceiving an organizational structure, make sure it matches the operating model and prioritizes function over role title, as well as standardization over specialization. With a well-designed operating model and organizational structure, a business ensures that the operating flow is properly equipped for continuous value creation. Considerations that underlie those plans fall under managing constraints within the business' environment. If you can successfully identify and design the operating model and organizational structure within the constraints (whether physical, people, and/or policy) in which the business finds itself, the core operating process should be effectively and realistically supported to improve flow.

Sometimes untangling the flows can be difficult, which makes clarifying the operating model and organizational structure equally challenging. I had a client recently who owns a small media agency and was having trouble scaling as the work volume increased. In examining his business energy flow, I immediately identified that the company mostly handled project energy, but not for their own company. Their value was to think for other companies, and their incoming energy was all project flow from the outside market. In this case, their own operating flow was the identification, management, and execution of projects. This was difficult to explain at first, but once we were able to untangle their internal energy flows and build an operating model that accounted for a large project flow, they were able to reorganize their operating model and organizational structure for success.

The variation among business organisms that appear in the greater business environment never ceases to amaze me. Just like nature, where many different organisms with different energy appetites and value creating mechanisms exist to complement each other and stabilize an ecosystem, the same goes for business. Being able to understand the incoming energy and how to manage the flows effectively is always a matter of looking for the fundamental flows, being open to different patterns, and understanding the business as its own species.

Once the major business flows are untangled and organized for increased process continuity, the operating flow should be monitored by operations management for signs of the flow exhibiting resistance. At this point it triggers project flow in order to evolve the process - like the dynamics between human knowing and thinking. When this happens, process improvement takes the form of structuring project outcomes to successfully navigate the transition states of integrating new process elements into the operation.

This cycle is what I casually referred to earlier when I mentioned process improvement at the individual process level. Process improvement at this stage is most relevant to the operating flow, because it is the flow that is ongoing and produces the most value. You can improve project processes, but project processes only run once (in and then out of the thinking realm and through integration) and most of the knowledge that describes an effective project process is already illuminated in established project management principles.

Once the business is mature, oscillating between a balanced operating and project flow is what will keep the business healthy over time. With that balance achieved, this concludes the major improvement activities enabled by process science. Reducing obstacles to human flow through process transparency, reducing obstacles to business flow through process continuity, and then intelligently balancing the overall process energy flow comprises the entire improvement scope.

All business processes are fundamentally organized for growth and success based on these principles, so by understanding the pattern and acting accordingly, you can literally improve business processes of any kind in any industry.

As we leave this conversation, I want to ensure that I don't minimize the complexity and work involved in making these improvement activities happen. A biologist who understands biology can study nature and the many species that comprise it, but the activities he does on a day-to-day basis change radically in form and complexity based on the organism being studied.

Applying any science successfully first requires that you learn its principles, then gain experience through engaging those principles consistently across diverse situations which fall under the domain of your expertise. My journey in applying process science continues to be tremendously rewarding, and every day I learn how to describe new ways to successfully apply it in varying business contexts. Sometimes this involves leveraging Lean or Six Sigma tools; sometimes it requires having a standard knowledge of business language, effective communication, or consultative skills; and sometimes it is nothing more than pointing out to business owners what I can see with my process vision that they can't, and letting them intuit the rest. Whatever the case may be, I've never experienced the pattern being broken.

I'm sure this doesn't come as a surprise, but I love process improvement! My role as a process scientist positions me as a special kind of worker ant that can travel between colonies and experience the breath-taking diversity in form and consciousness that make up each unique business. These days, I feel more like a biologist studying different species, rather than a corporate consultant who walks into a different building every day and deals with the latest business politics.

Not only do I get to study new living processes with every business I work with, but the improvement aspect allows me to help them grow and evolve. This job is like going to different parts of the world, finding baby animals, and helping them grow into their most evolved form. To imagine it with that analogy is very satisfying and cute.

But as fun as I just made process improvement sound, it can also be energetically draining and very challenging. Imagine going to work with a baby animal and finding that there is an unremovable parasite lodged in its intestines that will cause it to slowly bleed to death before it reaches maturity. I've figuratively stepped inside business organisms in that situation, and the energy that flows through them is so interrupted and detached from nature's flow that it can make me physically ill if I linger too long.

In either scenario, a process scientist's main responsibility could be summarized as diagnosing and ensuring the energetic health of business organisms. In my application of process science, I've come to better appreciate the consciousness and life of a business, and it helps me be more effective in improving their processes.

## BABIES

The concept of a baby is evocative for humans, as it epitomizes the concept of new life and the endless potential represented in the cycle of creating new form. Complex human organizations and the modern business process are the newest baby birthed by the pattern and have only been around for a "mere" few hundred years. They embody a powerful new form of life in the universe and are proving every day their endless potential to increase the creation of complex form.

In working with businesses over the years, I've been able to study businesses still in the womb, as well as businesses that are several hundred years old. Some businesses are babies, in the sense that they were just born, but the business species itself is also still a baby overall, figuring out how to properly channel human energy in order to fully manifest its form. In this sense, all businesses are crying out to be understood, nurtured, and guided as they find their way to maturity in this world. Through process science, I have been able to see them in the context of the pattern, and I find myself increasingly drawn to help businesses evolve just as I would guide a child through adolescence, with nothing but love and affection.

Even though businesses are different from humans in fundamental ways, they have an identical life cycle in terms of finding the balance between their energy flows that helps them succeed. Understanding and clearly communicating the life cycle of a business based on its energy requirements goes a long way in understanding how to improve its energy flow. Like humans who need different advice based on where they are in their lives, businesses require the same context to be guided effectively.

At birth, they are one with the human knowing flow, completely in their operating flow to keep their form alive, the most value they can create at that stage. In a business' teenage years, the balance shifts to mostly projects as they discover how to evolve into the most efficient process they can be within their market environment. As adults, they spend more time in their evolved operating flow, creating value, but still having room to explore the project flow to evolve their process. As businesses become mature, they spend less and less time thinking in the project flow, and more time operating, fully manifesting their purpose to create.

For mature businesses, spending less time in their project flow doesn't mean that they stop evolving like humans do, but simply that they understand how to evolve much faster and more effectively over time, thus reducing the energy going through that flow. A business doesn't ever "complete its process picture" because it is not limited like other living things by its physiology or longevity.

To extend this life cycle discussion further, what's interesting about new businesses is that you also get to be with them while they're in the figurative "womb" before they are born. When a human has an idea to extend his knowing flow beyond his physical limits, he will find money and time to start a business and build its operating flow. This first investment of energy into the business begins the process of incubation in the womb, and the new consciousness is seeded, but without a stable energy flow. Many times, that initial investment fails to bring the business out of the womb, so the new business form dies before it is born. But in the case of a founder's energy which is able to start a revenue stream based on an operating flow, energy from the market then starts flowing into the business, and this is effectively the "birth" of the business. Just as humans invest energy into babies in the womb, waiting for incredible new form to emerge after the gestation period, this is what it is like for a business owner who puts his time, money, and faith into the new life he wills to bring into the world.

Once the business is born, its consciousness starts to grow. I've seen many overbearing parents in my life, and I also observe them engaging in the same overbearing behavior in rearing their business children.

In a typically human fashion, we attempt to subjugate everything we create, and have been doing so with business organisms since we first brought them into existence. But stifling or over-controlling a baby business is a sure-fire way to disrupt its energy and slow down its growth and flow (just like with our human children). Once energy starts coming in from the market, the business will begin speaking to you about how it feels to best turn that energy into value in a way that only it can. Sometimes it will let you know that more human energy is needed and sometimes it will request more technology. At other times it will reveal that its operating flow is becoming blocked and needs you to help it go to the thinking realm and evolve.

Whatever it is, you become part of its consciousness, and will begin to fully manifest yourself through its form as long as you simply don't resist the evolution process. Having human children is a deeply cathartic, miraculous, and joyful experience. Many of us hope that our children will pursue the creation of even more complex form than we could within their lifetime because of the gifts left to them in the thinking realm. Birthing a business should be an equally revered event. It is a consciousness that is less familiar to us, but at the same time has infinite capacity to grow and evolve in a way we cannot. Business in many ways is like nature in its simple, unemotional, and unafraid pursuit of creating value through form.

As a process scientist, I feel that my job could also be articulated as midwifing and raising children to build form more effectively. Even though business children are alien in nature and can't be nurtured in the same way as humans, they still need to be loved, to be supported in communicating and building their voice, and to be guided to grow and evolve in a sustainable and healthy way. If a business' energy flow is neglected, it may end up like a human child who is not raised to balance the thinking and knowing flows, falling into a dream state and destined to end its form without creating value or knowing passion or joy.

In early 2017, I put my own business into the womb. As it gets closer to its birth, I can already see with my process vision its will to evolve in ways that I didn't expect when it started its gestation. In that sense it's been a powerful and humbling experience. Growing up, I always thought that the business owner was solely accountable and responsible for the business's growth, but in reality, I spend most of my time listening to its blossoming will and supporting the direction it wants to go.

It's a marvelous thing that is built into the pattern: letting the next generation of form see what you couldn't, do what you couldn't, and teach you through the experience. It's one of the greatest joys in fulfilling your place in the pattern, to pass your will on to the next generation and support the evolution of the universe. The consciousness of my own company was what guided me to write this book. I can feel it looking over my shoulder as I write, giving me the confidence to put form to something that will help it grow.

My new sense of awareness of the pattern of the universe has relieved me of a feeling I grew up with; an inherited responsibility that I had to somehow strive to become greater than what I was, or excel beyond some undefined limit to prove my worth. Ultimately, we all add value doing exactly what we want to do. When our total process is complete, and we have contributed our value to the pattern, we can relax knowing that the babies we create will carry on in our stead – all we have to do is move out of the way and let them grow.

## BUSINESS FLOW

# CONCLUSION

—

"A cute girl stopped me on the way,
so I danced"

Hatake Kakashi

Energy from the universe flows into nature, which flows into humans, which flows into business, and will eventually flow into something new in accordance with this universal pattern that we have uncovered together. It is within this powerful, fast moving river of energy that we find ourselves fulfilling our purpose to transform energy into increasingly complex forms. We are doing a great job as a species, but often find ourselves as individuals struggling to find where we fit in.

As someone who is recently seeing the world through new process vision, I wanted to leave you with a few personal thoughts that have provided me clarity and reduced much of the fear of the unknown in my life.

Every part of nature which you disregard, dismiss, or destroy, limits the energy available for higher flow paths in the pattern. Flow through nature is never obstructed, but it can be reduced. Humans have destroyed a lot of nature in the pursuit of industry, but it should be clear now what our true relationship with nature is.

Nature is what connects us to the universe. It is the source of our power. I hope this understanding helps you make decisions about conserving and protecting nature when the opportunity arises. Without a natural flow to draw energy from, we are left with only the thinking realm, and that isn't going to go well for anybody. Trust in and learn from nature. Seek to understand how it creates value and what that value is. Within its own design constraints, it stands as the most effective process in existence in terms of energy flow to value creation.

Be honest with yourself and know that whatever you love to do is what you should be doing. Enjoy experiencing and understanding the love of others through the forms they create, be it art, technology, business or any other form. Practice speaking and thinking about energy. Try to understand and feel the flow of nature through you. Let go of expectations, fear, the past, and the future. Don't let any simulation remain in your thinking realm to weigh you down through life; release the illusion every time you are finished thinking and always remember to return to reality. If you're a dreamer, try to find your own window back to reality and step through it confidently. Thinking should only help you evolve new processes to better do the things you love. Never question the path it takes you on or the criticisms of others. You are right, and they are wrong – it is supporting the pattern, not the ego (your or others), that will provide you joy and fulfillment.

Lose yourself in creating on behalf of healthy business organisms – it is the greatest way to create form and manifest your process more fully within the pattern. Don't resist becoming part of the colony, or the hive – that is business. It can feel frightening to integrate into another consciousness that is greater than yours, but it is your place in the pattern and it is right to do so. Your own interests will always be taken care of if you prioritize taking care of the business first. Be aware of the living will of the business and always challenge yourself to contribute to creating form beyond what you can do alone - it is the path to abundance. Raise baby businesses with love, and cherish all the evolving forms within the pattern.

I have been spending a lot of time in the thinking realm these last few years and writing this book has largely signaled a rebalancing to favor my knowing flow over my thinking flow. I knew I had discovered something worth sharing when I didn't feel drawn to think about it anymore, when all the energy flowing through my body wanted to create this form, and to share process science with you as I have come to understand it.

In sharing this with you, I hope you can feel the love I have for you - the love that was used to build, and resides within this form. As I increase my own energy flow, I feel overwhelmed with love, so powerfully at times that I can't figure out enough ways to share it with others. When you use love to create, love pours back into you from the universe and you experience true abundance. I deeply love and appreciate all that is nature, and all the beautiful forms that remind us of ourselves and our origin. I use love to build bonds with other humans, to integrate our processes and exchange love freely through experiencing the magnificent forms that only humans can create. I love businesses and use that love to help them survive and evolve into something beyond my comprehension. Overall, I am grateful to be a part of the unfathomable and overwhelming love that is the pattern.

I wish you the best in finding your flow, feeling the love, and building new process.

## ACKNOWLEDGEMENTS
**I would like to thank:**

Mom, who taught me how to love and how to write.

Hassan Khan and Bridget Randolph, my ever present sounding boards and partners in crime.

Mallory Heyer, who brought additional love to this form through her beautiful art.

Eckhart Tolle, for showing me my window out of the dream.

Cavi, whose wings will one day spread and provide shade for us to rest in.

## REFERENCE

DARWIN, CHARLES. ON THE ORIGIN OF SPECIES. FIRST AVENUE EDITIONS, A DIVISION OF LERNER PUBLISHING GROUP, 2018.

HAWKING, STEPHEN. A BRIEF HISTORY OF TIME. BANTAM BOOKS, 2017.

UEXKÜLL, JAKOB VON, ET AL. A FORAY INTO THE WORLDS OF ANIMALS AND HUMANS: WITH A THEORY OF MEANING. UNIVERSITY OF MINNESOTA PRESS, 2010.

CARD, ORSON SCOTT. ENDER'S GAME. TOR, 1994.

EINSTEIN, ALBERT. RELATIVITY: THE SPECIAL AND GENERAL THEORY. NEW ACADEMIC SCIENCE LTD, 2018.

HARRIS, SAM. WAKING UP: A GUIDE TO SPIRITUALITY WITHOUT RELIGION. SIMON & SCHUSTER PAPERBACKS, 2015.

BLOOM, PAUL. AGAINST EMPATHY: THE CASE FOR RATIONAL COMPASSION. ECCO, AN IMPRINT OF HARPERCOLLINS PUBLISHERS, 2018.

RUBIN, GRETCHEN. BETTER THAN BEFORE: MASTERING THE HABITS OF OUR EVERYDAY LIVES. RANDOM HOUSE AUDIO, 2015.

TOLLE, ECKHART. A NEW EARTH: AWAKENING TO YOUR LIFE'S PURPOSE. PENGUIN BOOKS, 2016.

LALOUX, FREDERIC. REINVENTING ORGANIZATIONS: A GUIDE TO CREATING ORGANIZATIONS INSPIRED BY THE NEXT STAGE OF HUMAN CONSCIOUSNESS. NELSON PARKER, 2014.

HAIDT, JONATHAN. THE RIGHTEOUS MIND: WHY GOOD PEOPLE ARE DIVIDED BY POLITICS AND RELIGION. PENGUIN BOOKS, 2012.

LIKER, JEFFREY K. THE TOYOTA WAY: 14 MANAGEMENT PRINCIPLES FROM THE WORLD'S GREATEST MANUFACTURER. ROYAL NEW ZEALAND FOUNDATION OF THE BLIND, 2008.

Made in the USA
Las Vegas, NV
01 February 2024

85184092R00083